PACIFIC NORTHWEST

THE ULTIMATE WINERY GUIDE

PACIFIC NORTHWEST

THE ULTIMATE WINERY GUIDE

OREGON, WASHINGTON, AND BRITISH COLUMBIA

by Christina Melander

photographs by Jānis Miglavs

foreword by Kathy Casey

CHRONICLE BOOKS
SAN FRANCISCO

DEDICATION

For the Northwestern pioneers, old and new, who buck conventional wisdom and continue to coax incredible wines from unlikely places.

CHRISTINA

As I talked with the grape pickers in the cool morning air of the vineyards and listened to the winemakers talk oak and sugar, it reminded me that we come to this world to do particular work. That work is the purpose, and each is specific to the person. If we don't do it, it's as though the priceless fruit from the best 80-year-old vines was left to rot in the field. Thus I dedicate this work to the One who makes it all happen.

JĀNIS

Library of Congress Cataloging-in-Publication Data available.
ISBN-10: 0-8118-5529-5
ISBN-13: 978-0-8118-5529-7

Design by *Scott Thorpe*
Typeset in Atma, Noble, and Serifa

Manufactured in China.

Distributed in Canada by Raincoast Books
9050 Shaughnessy Street
Vancouver, British Columbia V6P 6E5

10 9 8 7 6 5 4 3 2 1

Chronicle Books LLC
680 Second Street
San Francisco, California 94107
www.chroniclebooks.com

ACKNOWLEDGMENTS

For Zach—driver, marathon taster, tireless traveler, bodyguard, and husband—who cooked and coddled so I could get this book done. Special thanks to fabulous friends Audrey, Brooke, and Tina, who endured my stressed-out ranting. And much gratitude to my nurturing family, who always encourage me to try new things.

CHRISTINA MELANDER

Naturally, I need to thank my wife Eddi; my kids Daniel, Ryan, and Veronica; and my grandkids Jose, Eddie, Michael, and little Veronica for putting up with my weeks of wanderings and my getting up at 3:30 in the morning to get that first-light photograph. Also I need to thank all of the dedicated field workers and enthusiastic winemakers who not only gave me insights into the special world of crafting wine but also waited patiently when I asked if I could take just one more photograph. And I need to thank the force, spirit or luck that was constantly with me to make sunlight momentarily break through the leaden blanket of Pacific Northwest rain clouds to touch the vineyard just as I clicked the shutter. But most of all, I need to thank the One who owns my every breath and moment.

JĀNIS MIGLAVS

Contents

Wow! The Northwest wine scene has flourished in the past few years. No longer are we recognized just for Chardonnay, Pinot Noir, and Merlot; distinctive and unusual grape varieties are being planted all over our diverse growing areas. Today we see Tempranillo, Viognier, and Pinot Auxerrois; Cabernet Franc and Syrah are now mainstays on our dinner tables. It's not hard to find a new favorite wine every week. As a Seattle native, I have had the good fortune to see the region's wine industry blossom into its current status as a world-class wine producer. There are now hundreds of wineries in Washington, Oregon, and British Columbia.

This book is a great resource for locals and visitors alike. Christina's gregarious personality, food connections, and experience as a reviewer have served her admirably in preparing this guide. In her easygoing style, she shares with you her well-informed enthusiasm for the region and its wines.

The Pacific Northwest is known for its fabulous foods and culinary bounty. Sweet Dungeness crab; juicy, luscious berries; earthy wild forest mushrooms; briny, ice-cold oysters; lush, buttery salmon; crisp-snapping apples…do these sound a lot like descriptions of wines? Of course! Wine is a food, too. And this enchanting libation certainly makes magic when it's paired with a perfect food match. To me, wine is like a meal's jewelry. Highlighting and accentuating the entire ensemble, wine heightens food flavors to their peak.

Probably one of my most memorable wine-and-food pairing experiences was a dinner at the home of winemaker friends in Eastern Washington. They had just returned from California, where the family had been abalone diving. We had thin slices of abalone quickly seared in a pan over a hot grill in the yard. My husband, John, and I had brought fresh Columbia River sturgeon caviar that a "way-foodie" friend had given us as a special treat for our anniversary; we dolloped the caviar on thin crostini and dotted it with crème fraîche. We nibbled these delicacies while sipping our friends' personal stash of experimental sparkling wine. Then we moved on to local lamb chops grilled over rosemary branches. The meat was topped with deep-red cherry salsa made with fruit just picked from their field out back; new potatoes, salad from the garden, and, of course, their luscious Merlot accompanied the lamb. This was one of those wine-and-food marriages that I will savor forever in my mind.

I certainly have other fantastic wine memories. Popping oysters open on a cold, rainy beach on British Columbia's Vancouver Island and slurping them down with a bottle of crisp Sauvignon Blanc: naked oysters and chilled wine, divine. Sitting with new friends on the Spanish Steps in Rome and passing around a three-dollar bottle of tasty Italian red wine; our

11

little gathering didn't speak one another's languages, but we all spoke the international language of wine, and we had a wonderful time.

Sharing a great bottle of wine with friends, a lover, or family can create an everlasting memory. It may be as crazy-casual as John's and my drive back west from a stint living in New York. After a long, long day on the road in Wyoming—and carrying a copy of an excellent small-town U.S. foodie guide—we just *had* to pick up some ribs at a famous barbecue restaurant. Our packages in tow, we settled into the only "inn" in town—the place looked like it was out of a 1950s Lucy and Desi movie. We spread out our feast of sexy local "Q" and relished it with a bottle of 1982 Château Margaux—which we drank from plastic glasses. And it was one of the best wine experiences I have ever had.

This just goes to show you that a grand bottle of wine need not be appreciated only in a fancy-pants environment. Wine should be enjoyed by all, with no pretense and pomp—but with robust enthusiasm!

I hope that, with Christina guiding you, you'll get out and experience our fantastic array of remarkable wineries; that you'll have a chance to connect with the winemakers over tastings and through inspiring and informative conversations; and that this book will acquire lots of notes, dog-eared pages, and, of course, a few stains from much-enjoyed wines. This guide will lead you to hidden gems and not-to-be-missed spots in unknown territory, and give you the inside scoop on the specialties of each winery and the faces and personalities behind the wines.

Cheers!

KATHY CASEY

Introduction

While visiting wineries in Oregon's celebrated northern Willamette Valley, I wandered into a musty used-book shop in McMinnville and came across a sturdy little hardcover called *A Guide to Good Wine* by J. W. Mahoney. The 1972 edition of a book originally published twenty years earlier in London, it featured beautiful hand-drawn maps of famed European wine regions. Black-and-white snapshots of girls in sunbonnets chewing fat bunches of grapes were, well, almost racy. In other words, it seemed well worth five dollars, even if the prose turned out to be hokey. But the writing, though of course dated, proved to be quite compelling. One passage really caught my attention:

In the New World, where the vine is also grown commercially, the knowledge and appreciation of wine is steadily and rapidly increasing, but in general the wines are mainly copies of the better-known European wines, and, so far as the writer knows, none of the new countries has yet produced a native wine with its own special characteristics and qualities which will bear comparison with the choicest growths of the Old World. An Australian burgundy, a South African hock, a Chilean Riesling may all be wines of excellent quality and flavour, but they cannot be an exact copy of their European counterparts, for the conditions of growth in Europe cannot be duplicated. The same grape, the same method of cultivation, the same method of production may be used, but the grower cannot duplicate the exact soil conditions or the distribution and amount of sun, rain and wind, and these will always cause differences which will be reflected in the final product.

My, how times have changed.

Initially, New World winemakers, first in California, then in cooler climes to the north, did model their wines on the great examples of Bordeaux, Alsace, Burgundy, and the Rhône. Through much trial and error and a determination to understand the relationship between grape and place, winemakers realized that, as Mahoney wrote, they could not replicate Old World wines—but they could make something just as good. Or better. The Northwest embodies the commitment to figuring out which grapes grow best in a given patch of dirt and to crafting wines evocative of the land. Washington's Syrah stands apart from California's; a winemaker in Dundee, Oregon, strives to make Pinot Noir that reflects the red Jory soil it sprang from, not to mimic Burgundy.

Growers in Oregon, Washington, and British Columbia benefited somewhat from research in California, the first established West Coast wine region. But these northerly neighbors have little in common with California—or even with one another—when it comes to climate, soil, rainfall, altitude, and the numerous other niggling factors that affect grapes. Conditions vary wildly from region to region: two vineyard plots within a mile of each other can yield very different results. Winegrowers are constantly appraising land, testing clones and methods, and refining their approach to produce exceptional fruit. As winemakers will tell you, great wine is made in the vineyard.

And the experimentation continues. In the Northwest, the earliest vinifera vineyards were planted in the 1960s. Forty years is a brief track record compared to Europe's centuries of growing and making wine. But today, hundreds of grape varieties—some just in test plots, others on a mass scale—are grown in the hills and valleys of the Pacific Northwest. There are well-known varietals: Pinot Noir and Pinot Gris in Oregon; Merlot and Cabernet Sauvignon in Washington; and Gewürztraminer and Riesling in British Columbia. But winemakers are also playing

A friend recently asked me if it's fun to visit wineries. I was floored. While researching this book, I spent months doing little else. I wouldn't have maintained that schedule if it hadn't been enjoyable. "I have a vision of filing into a crowded tasting room and being treated badly by indifferent pourers," my friend elaborated. If this woman, a young, bright journalist who loves wine, harbors such an impression, I can only imagine what the wine-drinking public at large thinks.

How did New World wineries, founded by pioneers who sought authenticity and dismissed pretense, earn a reputation for snobbery? Is it a result of years of tolerating waiters and wine stewards who haughtily corrected our mispronunciations of French wine names? Was it that infamous *Sideways* scene in which Miles is refused another glass of wine at a fancy showpiece winery that confirmed our worst fears? Are high prices to blame?

Whatever the reasons, visiting a few Northwest wineries should put to rest any perception of wineries as unwelcoming clubs for the elite. Touring wineries in Oregon, Washington, and British Columbia is a laid-back affair. Yes, there are grand properties modeled on Bordeaux chateaux, but you won't feel out of place padding across the Italian tile flooring in flip-flops. And for every sprawling hilltop estate, there are fifty pocket wineries where the owners will be the ones pouring and sharing stories behind the tasting bar.

Tasting rooms here are convivial and casual, not imposing. Winery staff are generally friendly and eager to introduce and discuss their varietals and blends. In dozens of interviews, I heard owners, managers, and winemakers express again and again how much they welcome curious visitors. If you have questions, ask! Your interest may lead to the barrel cellars, where winemakers are only too happy to extract samples of wine at various stages of maturity, or to a sip of delicious limited-edition port. The point of touring wineries, after all, is to learn. Don't feel that you should have all the answers prior to your visit—who better to teach you a thing or two than the people who make, think about, and drink wine for a living?

around with grapes most people have never heard of, including Pinot Auxerrois, Rousanne, and Albariño.

For visitors—even wine-savvy visitors—the Pacific Northwest holds many surprises. Wineries have proliferated at a breakneck rate since the late 1990s, and a collaborative spirit among winemakers, vineyard managers, chefs, and independent wine distributors makes the industry strong and unified. But as large and sophisticated as the industry has become, it still is composed primarily of small boutique producers and exudes a grassroots feel.

There are only a couple of gargantuan commercial wineries. Most houses are craft producers striving to make varietally true wines. A growing number of independent winemakers eschew traditional bricks-and-mortar wineries of their own, renting space within larger operations or having grapes pressed for them to create a few hundred cases of wine. Winery tasting rooms range from teensy and rustic to enormous and extravagant, affording visitors vastly different experiences. Fighting through crowds to get a glass of wine is rare: in Northwest wine country, there's plenty of room—and wine—for everyone.

WINERY SELECTION

With more than eight hundred wineries in Oregon, Washington, and British Columbia, how to choose just thirty? It wasn't easy. This book's editor, photographer, and I started by narrowing the field to wineries that have tasting rooms and are open to the public year-round. That ruled out a tremendous number of stellar wineries, but it wouldn't be any fun if we didn't let you make discoveries of your own. One thrill of cruising country roads is stumbling upon a little winery you've never heard of, which just might offer some terrific wines.

Second, we sought to represent the various wine-producing regions spread throughout the states (in British Columbia, we focused solely on the Okanagan Valley, the province's largest winemaking zone). We selected wineries that stood out for their informative tours, unusual events, compelling architecture, and gorgeous settings. Striking a balance between little-known bohemian wineries and larger operations with name recognition was crucial. Finally, we chose wineries that boasted both intriguing stories and incredible wines.

USING THIS GUIDE

Use this book to get acquainted with the Northwest wine scene. It should serve as a jumping-off point for your exploration of these distinctive stomping grounds that nurture both grapes and wine lovers. If you journey to Chelan, Washington, to visit Tsillan Cellars, by all means check out the other wineries clustered around expansive Lake Chelan. While touring Argyle or Adelsheim in Oregon's dense Willamette Valley, let tasting-room managers direct you to a few of the many other wineries in Yamhill County. When you travel to the Okanagan Valley, build time into your itinerary to amble along British Columbia's Naramata Bench, home to several interesting mom-and-pop wineries.

Your forays may take you through arid canyon-lands, lush rainforest terrain, hazelnut groves, towns stuck in bygone eras, strip-mall sprawl, and acres upon acres of tidy, shoulder-high vines. These rugged western lands pack a hefty dose of natural beauty, a reason enterprising vintners settle down in their dramatic valleys. You'll encounter both familiar wines such as Chardonnay, Pinot Noir, and Syrah and eclectic varietals along the lines of Pinot Auxerrois, Lemberger, and Tempranillo. And you'll meet people with stories as varied as the wines the region produces. The Pacific Northwest is fresh turf in the annals of winemaking, and the turf holds much promise. Keep your eye on it—and enjoy the view. ❧

21

Just as people travel differently, they tour differently. Some people seize a cloudless day on a whim, jump in the car, and stop at the first wineries in their path. Others plan entire vacations around wineries of interest, drafting precise itineraries to allow for maximum visitation. But most people probably fall somewhere between these poles. A combination of planning ahead and winging it is an excellent recipe for a fulfilling spin through wine country. To that end, here are some pointers, a primer on tasting-room protocol, and insight into what you can expect on the winery trail.

PLANNING YOUR VISITS

Whether you sip or spit when tasting, do not delude yourself by thinking you can power through a half-dozen wineries in one day. Far from constituting an idyllic getaway in wine country, a stacked schedule will leave you exhausted. It's much more enjoyable to spend time getting to know a winery—chatting with staff, attending a tour, or lingering over a picnic lunch—than to sprint from tasting room to tasting room, only to whip through a few glasses of wine.

Proximity permitting, start by visiting three wineries over the course of a day, stopping at additional estates if they catch your eye. Consider allowing time for nonvinous attractions, too, such as the Evergreen Air Museum in McMinnville, Oregon, the Ginkgo Petrified Forest in central Washington, or a detour through downtown Kelowna in British Columbia. And don't forget to eat! If you are on a rigorous schedule, it's wise to pack snacks—fruit, nuts, granola bars, cheese and crackers—in case you don't have time for a sit-down lunch. (You'll also want to bring plenty of water—wine is dehydrating.) Some wineries sell picnic items in their tasting rooms, while several estates in the Okanagan Valley have inviting on-site restaurants (as noted in the profile sidebars). Regional dining recommendations can be found in the next chapter.

Large wineries can afford staffing for regular tours, but many small operations ask that visitors make appointments for tours in advance (again, see the information provided in profile sidebars). Doing so may not always fit into your plans, but keep in mind that some of the best tours do require reservations.

WHAT TO EXPECT

My hunch is that more people would visit wineries if they knew what to expect—and knew what was expected of them as guests. It's really pretty simple. The tasting room is your main point of contact, though larger wineries have guest reception areas, lobbies, or concierge stations too. If tours are offered, they usually conclude with a tasting, a natural progression from learning about how the wines are made to tasting the results. Some wineries favor self-guided tours and provide accompanying literature or signage to enhance your understanding as you amble around the facility.

What you witness at a winery will depend on the season. Just like any other agriculture-based business, wineries and vineyards change throughout the year. In the spring, wineries release new bottlings and vines bud and leaf out. Summer is for celebrating, hosting events, and preparing the winery for harvest by readying equipment and moving wine from tanks to barrels. In the vineyard, grapes emerge and ripen in the extended sunlight. Autumn is the busiest time of year. Pickers race to get grapes in, and winery crews rush to sort, de-stem, and crush or macerate fruit, transforming it into juice. Juice is then moved into bins and tanks for fermentation. Visiting wineries in fall is fun and informative, providing a glimpse into the workings of a vineyard or winery; some operations even stage harvest events that allow guests to play a small role in the winemaking process. As fall turns into winter, newly fermented juice goes into stainless steel tanks or barrels, settling in for aging. Vines go dormant and are cut back in preparation for next year's crop.

25

Tasting wine should be fun, interesting, rewarding, revelatory—anything but terrifying. Yet paranoia and anxiety often besiege us when it's time to taste. *Should I spit or swallow? Do I really stick my nose all the way into the glass? Will I look funny when I spit? What if I miss?* Relax. The purpose of tasting wine is to figure out what you like and discover new favorites. No one is looking for a performance.

If tours aren't available or you decide not to take part in one, grab a spot at the tasting bar and ask what's being poured that day. Some wineries post lists of featured wines, including tasting notes and prices. Cost varies: some wineries don't charge guests to taste, some charge only for reserve or limited-edition selections, and others charge a set fee or a fee that is refundable if you purchase wine to take home.

Pourers will commence with their lightest-bodied wine, a white such as Pinot Gris or Sauvignon Blanc if the winery makes whites, or a Sangiovese or Pinot Noir if only reds are on offer. Each successive wine will be weightier or more tannic as you work your way through a tasting. If the winery is pouring sweet dessert wines, those will come last. Advancing from delicate to powerful wines ensures a relatively fresh palate and prevents the nuances of Viognier from being clouded by the boldness of Cabernet Sauvignon.

Tasting protocol goes something like this, but you are under no obligation to follow it:

LOOK

One of the cool things about tasting a lot of wine is noticing differences in color. Wines are often lovely to behold, so take a peek. Some people like to hold the glass at an angle against a white background to best observe a wine's hue.

SWIRL

You may feel silly swirling, but don't skimp on this step. Moving the liquid around releases aromas as alcohol evaporates and carries the wine's scents toward your nose.

26

SMELL

We can identify thousands of aromas, but we can taste only four flavors (sweet, sour, salty, and bitter), so how the wine smells is pretty crucial to our enjoyment of it. The idea is to get a good, long whiff of wine, which is easiest if you're close to the stuff. Put your nose into the glass and breathe in deeply.

TASTE

This is where we get fouled up. Professional tasters pull air into their mouths when sampling wine—again to aerate it and to splash it over various taste receptors on the tongue. If you want to try this, practice at home first, or you might induce a bit of a coughing fit. You can either spit or swallow at this point; the choice is yours. (Not all tasting rooms set out receptacles, but you can always ask for one.) You can also just consume a portion of your pour and release the rest into the dump bucket. There's no need to rinse your glass with water between tastes.

APPRAISE

Try to discern key flavors, texture, and balance—i.e., the interplay of fruit, acidity, and tannins. Recognizing what you like and dislike, not just whether a wine appeals, sets you on the path toward understanding your tastes. Jotting down impressions to refer to later is also helpful. ✌

Serious wine connoisseurs might regard wine as a venerated liquid meant to be savored on its own. The rest of us like to drink it with food.

Consuming wine with meals makes both dinner and drink taste better, especially when we hit on a harmonious match: Pinot Noir that smooths out the slight gaminess of wild salmon, or a cool, dry Riesling that tempers fiery lamb vindaloo. The bounty of the Pacific Northwest—from cultivated heirloom tomatoes to mushrooms loosened from damp forest earth to handmade goat cheese to shellfish snatched from Puget Sound—presents ample opportunity to discover ideal pairings with a vast lineup of regional wines.

It's interesting to contemplate whether wine drives regional cuisine or vice versa. Is it coincidence that aromatic Germanic white wines thrive in British Columbia and partner fabulously with the plentiful seafood of the north Pacific? Do you put down to chance the undeniable compatibility of Pinot Noir and Oregon berries, hazelnuts, and foraged mushrooms? Or is it simply that shared soil, climate, and topography produce commonalities in local foods and wines, making them naturally fit partners?

Northwest cuisine emerged only in the past twenty-five years and is still being defined. Greg Higgins, chef-owner of his eponymous Portland restaurant, is a noted founder of the movement to cook with local, seasonally available ingredients: "I was cooking in Seattle in 1980 and I could see interest in local foods picking up, but chefs hadn't jumped in whole hog. Between 1980 and 1990, I began to look for growers and tried to find regular channels for produce so I could execute a type of seed-to-table cuisine." Thanks to the efforts of like-minded chefs, farmers, and food activists, those channels are well established in Oregon and Washington today, fostering a style of cooking that is ecologically sustainable and bursting with the articulated flavors we most crave during a given season: soul-satisfying squash and root vegetables in fall and winter, delicate salad greens and perfumed berries in summer.

The infrastructure necessary to support seasonally propelled cooking is not yet as sophisticated in British Columbia's Okanagan Valley. "The bounty here is great, but the distribution is not," says Heidi Noble, founder of Joie Farm Cooking School in Naramata. Noble believes the food scene here is still in its infancy, due in part to the area's relatively sparse population and the seasonality of the Okanagan wine industry. "We don't have the population to support many fine restaurants year-round, so it's tough for chefs to make a go of it." There's reason to believe restaurants will catch up with wineries, however. More young entrepreneurs like Heidi and her husband, Michael Dinn—both trained sommeliers who produce Joie wines in addition to running the cooking school—are moving to the area, building a foundation for an exciting gastronomic destination.

Northwest cuisine isn't built on a long-standing tradition of ingredients and recipes. Native tribes grilled salmon on alder planks and harvested berries, but their food preparations bore little resemblance to modern regional cooking. "Native cooking was pretty rudimentary and lacked seasoning. There's not much there that would get our juices flowing," Higgins explains. Like Oregon, Washington, and British Columbia winemakers, chefs are creating something completely unique to the area. An absence of heritage is an opportunity, not a hindrance, freeing these artisans to lay down their own rules—or, more likely, to avoid rules altogether. ❧

OREGON

Ashland

Amuse Restaurant / 541.488.9000
15 N. First Street / dinner

Exacting French technique and wide-ranging West Coast ingredients come together in this elegant urban restaurant. The cheese course is given its due, though warm beignets with crème anglaise and berry jam may prove too tempting to bypass. Oregon, Washington, California, France, and Germany are all well represented on the wine list.

Black Sheep Pub & Restaurant / 541.482.6414
51 N. Main Street / lunch and dinner

This is the cool British pub of your dreams—right in southern Oregon. There are no ingratiating gimmicks here. You'll wonder how they got the bar, airy and cozy at the same time, so pitch-perfect. And the food is as good as the Guinness.

New Sammy's Cowboy Bistro / 541.535.2779
2210 S. Pacific Highway, Talent / dinner

Strange name, amazing restaurant. New Sammy's is a cult favorite, attracting savvy foodies from far and wide. Located just outside Ashland at the crossroads of Talent, it offers gastronomic delight to all who can find the place. The building is a crummy-looking cottage with no sign, but inside, the seven-table gem oozes charm. The ever-changing prix-fixe meal is mesmerizing.

Standing Stone Brewing Company / 541.482.2448
101 Oak Street / lunch and dinner

Sometimes you just want a beer. Standing Stone offers its own great brews and a host of others, plus satisfying pub fare that exceeds expectations. The convivial, easy-going atmosphere makes this a smart choice for families or groups.

Carlton

Cuvee Restaurant / 503.852.6555
214 W. Main St. / dinner plus weekend brunch in summer

Alsace-native chef Gilbert Henry made his mark in Portland with Winterbourne Restaurant, preparing classic French dishes with Northwest seafood. He continues that tradition at Cuvee, but offers a broader menu that is as likely to include bouillabaisse as a juicy steak.

Dayton

Joel Palmer House / 503.864.2995
600 Ferry Street / dinner

For some epicures, the Joel Palmer House is a bigger draw than Yamhill County's wineries. The stately restaurant is legendary for its preoccupation with foraged mushrooms; diners can request a five-course "mushroom madness" menu or order à la carte, choosing dishes such as roasted elk loin, beef stroganoff with mushrooms, or crab cakes in a porcini-chipotle sauce.

Dundee

The Dundee Bistro / 503.554.8068
100-A S.W. Seventh Street / lunch and dinner

A feature of the seasonal, Northwest-inspired menu is a large selection of Oregon wines by the half-bottle, a nice size for those feeling a little burned-out on wine tasting. A party atmosphere pervades the spacious dining room, and eclectic, colorful dishes highlight regional items such as Carlton pork, Puget Sound clams, and Painted Hills beef.

Dundee Pizza Company / 503.538.8112
575 S.W. Highway 99W / lunch and dinner

Not that many lunch spots exist in Dundee or the surrounding area. This one doesn't look like much from the outside, and ambience is not its strong suit, but

32

the pies are above average. A personal-sized pizza (big enough for two) will save you after a busy morning of tasting.

Tina's / 503.538.8880
760 Highway 99W / lunch and dinner
A mainstay of the Yamhill County dining scene, Tina's presents consistently fine dishes made with local ingredients. Here you might find pepper-crusted ahi tuna with braised fennel, a robust pork loin sandwich, buttermilk onion rings, or sweet roasted-corn soup, which derives its rich consistency from natural cream of corn. The restaurant has a relaxed, dressed-down air at lunchtime, when meals cost two-thirds less than their evening counterparts.

Eugene

Ambrosia Restaurant & Bar / 541.342.4141
174 E. Broadway / lunch and dinner
Warm and stylish, Ambrosia can take the edge off a chilly, damp day with its welcoming attitude and regional Italian specialties. The large menu ranges from lamb-stuffed sweet onions to duck risotto to numerous thin-crust pizzas. An extensive wine list showcases Italian and Northwest wines, with special attention paid to Pinot Noir.

Campbell House Inn / 541.343.1119
252 Pearl Street / dinner
This refined B&B opens its dining room to the public for dinner, serving a small, well-executed menu in a romantic setting. The wine list tilts toward Oregon, but the ambience is pure Europe.

Marché / 541.342.3612
296 E. Fifth Avenue / lunch and dinner
An exemplar of Northwest cuisine, lovely Marché is the anchor of Eugene's lively Fifth Street Market. Preparations like wood-oven-fired Chinook salmon with horseradish crème fraîche, crab napoleon layered with Oregon mushrooms and truffles, and roasted beet salad with Rogue Creamery blue cheese nicely show off the bounty of the region. Also in the market is Marché Café, a casual quick-stop alternative serving breakfast and lunch fare.

Steelhead Brewing Company / 541.686.2739
199 E. Fifth Avenue / lunch and dinner
A burger can be a beautiful thing, especially after a long afternoon of tasting in the nearby Lorane Valley. Steelhead delivers everything you crave in a brewpub: reliable, hunger-curbing fare, a range of expertly crafted beers, and a fun, rollicking vibe.

McMinnville

Bistro Maison / 503.474.1888
729 E. Third Street / lunch and dinner
Outfitted with barrel-back chairs, gilt-framed mirrors, and a patio festooned with impatiens, homey Bistro Maison is a smash hit with locals and tourists alike. The food is classic *cuisine de grand-mère*, all coarse pâté, smooth duck confit, and garlicky *moules*. It's one of those good-time restaurants you're always searching for—where the mood is convivial and the dishes spot-on.

Harvest Fresh Grocery & Deli / 503.472.5740
251 N.E. Third Street / lunch
Right in downtown McMinnville, this is a great place to stock up on fruit, cheeses, and snacks. Grab a table by the magazine rack or pad your picnic basket with deli fare, including appealing sandwiches and prepared noodle dishes and salads.

La Rambla Restaurant & Bar / 503.435.2126
238 N.E. Third Street / lunch and dinner
A relative newcomer to wine country, La Rambla offers a tasty changeup from Northwest cuisine: Spanish tapas. Curvy blown-glass pendant lamps set the tone for a sexy dining space, the ideal environment for savoring a bottle off one of the most extensive lists of Oregon Pinot Noir to be found anywhere.

Nick's Italian Café / 503.434.4471
521 N.E. Third Street / dinner

Ask anyone in McMinnville to recommend a restaurant and he'll invariably point you to Nick's, the town's most beloved and venerable eatery. The homemade pasta is lighter than Pinot Gris, and the lasagna is irresistible. Diners can choose the prix-fixe menu or order à la carte.

Red Fox Bakery / 503.434.5098
328 N.E. Evans Street / breakfast and lunch

The Red Fox makes a wide range of artisanal loaves, with daily specials ranging from cornmeal-molasses to semolina. It's a great destination for picnic goodies, and there's also room to sit down for a light breakfast or hearty gourmet sandwich. Save room for inch-thick chocolate chip–pumpkin seed cookies.

Newberg

The French Bear / 503.538.2609
107 S. College Street / breakfast, lunch, and dinner

Plan ahead for a picnic and pick up boxed lunches at the French Bear, a welcoming deli-bakery in downtown Newberg. Serving up Dutch babies (pancakes) and oatmeal for breakfast, the expanded café prepares sandwiches along the lines of capicola-and-provolone on focaccia, meaty salads, and killer brownies for dining in or take-away, plus casual bistro dinners. It's an affordable godsend in an area known for high-end special-occasion restaurants.

The Painted Lady / 503.538.3850
201 S. College Street / dinner

Basil-fed escargot, anyone? This Yamhill County newcomer delights diners with herbaceous snails, exquisite seasonal vegetables, and farmstead cheeses. Diners may choose the five-course tasting menu or build a meal of any three courses from the prix-fixe menu. The elegantly renovated Victorian-era house provides an intimate setting for the lengthy but expertly paced dinners. There's a full bar, creative Champagne cocktails, and a well-edited list of Northwest wines.

Panaderia y Videos Gonzales / 503.538.0306
615 E. First Street / lunch and dinner

Gonzales offers seriously good Mexican fare, including top-notch *carnitas* and *asada*. Baked goods are made on the premises, so *tortas* (sandwiches) are a good bet. This is the place to go when you're on the go or your wallet is hurting from that last case purchase.

WASHINGTON

Richland

Atomic Ale Brewpub & Eatery / 509.946.5465
1015 Lee Boulevard / lunch and dinner

This casual, good-humored restaurant draws its name from the nearby Hanford Site, where the U.S. government produced plutonium to build a line of defense during the Cold War. Items like Half-Life Hefeweizen and Chocolate Containment Cake wryly jab at this legacy. Wood-fired pizza is the specialty, but massive sandwiches, bountiful salads, and, of course, the beer all satisfy.

Bookwalter Winery / 509.627.5000
894 Tulip Lane / light lunch and dinner

A highly regarded winery dating from 1983, Bookwalter boasts a chic bistro at its inviting winery. The bistro promotes Washington farmstead cheeses (plus a few from New York and California), introducing guests to wonderful goat Gruyère, salty chèvre with orange zest and pecans, and Old Chatham Camembert. Other light fare, including cured meats, spreads, nuts, dried fruit, and artisan chocolates, perfectly complements the cheeses.

Stevenson

Big River Grill / 509.427.4888
192 S.W. Second Street / lunch and dinner

Fortifying food in a tavern setting is always a welcome sight on the winery trail. Settle in for hefty burgers, excellent club sandwiches, and friendly service while your eyes comb the vintage license plates and regional artifacts festooning the walls.

Walking Man Brewing / 509.427.5520
240 S.W. First Street / dinner

Give your palate a break with a beer flight. Walking Man offers a tasting tray with four-ounce pours of its ten rotating beers, all crafted with a fanatic's devotion. Individual pizzas, salads, and standard pub fare provide ballast.

Walla Walla

26brix Restaurant / 509.526.4075
207 W. Main Street / dinner and bar menu
(breakfast and lunch Sunday)

A stunner of a restaurant, 26brix is known for three things: its incomparable six-course chef's menu, an over-the-top fifty-two-dollar burger, and the spirited conversation that flows when winemakers and cellar rats congregate in the bar. Actually, it's known for much more, but there's not enough room here to enumerate the dishes and flourishes that make the place so special. Just go.

Creek Town Café / 509.522.4777
1129-D S. Second Avenue / lunch and dinner

Tasting-room staff at Walla Walla wineries often point visitors to this endearing café that emphasizes—you guessed it—goods from local growers and purveyors. A lengthy list of wines by the glass provides a good introduction to area wines. Save room for dessert.

Whitehouse-Crawford Restaurant / 509.525.2222
55 W. Cherry Street / dinner and bar menu

Situated in a renovated planing mill, a beautiful building the restaurant saved from demolition, Whitehouse-Crawford was the first dining establishment to draw serious foodie interest to Walla Walla. It continues to offer gorgeous Northwest cuisine with various international twists and turns.

Woodinville

The Barking Frog / 425.424.2999
14580 N.E. 145th Street / breakfast, lunch, and dinner
Situated in the welcoming Willows Lodge, the wine-themed Barking Frog promises seasonality with a side of fun. The bold, far-flung wine list is organized by descriptors to which diners really relate: Glacial and Bubbly; Wow; and Archaic, Dusty, and Expensive as Hell. Terrine of duck confit, accented by kumquat puree and pulled-from-the-hive honeycomb, typifies the restaurant's creative flavor arrangements.

The Herbfarm / 425.485.5300
14590 N.E. 145th Street / dinner
A dining experience unlike any other, a meal here begins with an informative stroll through the name-sake garden, where your leader will espouse the restaurant's cooking philosophy. The four-hour odyssey includes nine courses featuring the best from artisanal producers throughout the Northwest and five or six wines to match. This is a worthy once-in-a-lifetime indulgence.

Lowell-Hunt Garden Café / 425.398.5224
13625 N.E. 175th Street / lunch and meals to go
Talented Seattle caterers Jonathan Hunt and Russell Lowell bring their signature farm-fresh cooking to the masses at this informal café. A favorite among Woodinville workers, Lowell-Hunt is an ideal spot to grab a quick sandwich and cookie during a day's winery tour.

BRITISH COLUMBIA
Please see the British Columbia winery profiles, starting on page 97, for additional restaurants.

Kelowna

Fresco Restaurant & Lounge / 250.868.8805
1560 Water Street / dinner
A very bright spot in downtown Kelowna, Fresco celebrates regional seafood, meats, produce, and cheeses with irresistible concoctions. Dishes such as Okanagan pork three ways (grilled tenderloin, pork-belly-stuffed potato croquettes, and smoked hock and white bean stew) are tirelessly inventive. Be advised that desserts like double-chocolate mashed-potato brioche with raspberry sorbet will seriously test your willpower.

Naramata

Naramata Heritage Inn & Spa / 250.496.6808
3625 First Street / lunch and dinner
Situated in a tiny village on the east side of Lake Okanagan, this restored 1908 Mission-style inn offers peaceful luxury lodging—and some great meals. Choose between the polished Rove Oven Dining Room and the appealingly rustic Cobblestone Wine Bar & Restaurant for hearth-baked bread with exquisite artisan cheese from nearby Poplar Grove (also a winery), wild game dishes, and an impressive selection of B.C. wines.

Penticton

Theo's Restaurant / 250.492.4019
687 Main Street / lunch and dinner
Dinner at Theo's makes you feel like you're part of the family—the Theodosakis family, who have kept locals in souvlaki for more than twenty-five years. It's a spectacularly welcoming restaurant, with fires blazing in winter and generous patio seating on the foliage-covered courtyard in summer. Bring your appetite for fried chicken livers and baked lamb shoulder.

BLOOM: POLLINATE OR PERISH

After months of dormancy during chilly, wet winters, vines reawaken. Buds swell on the gnarled, brown canes, revealing the first green of spring. It's a fascinating time to walk through a vineyard. Each shoot holds a set pattern of growth, and as it elongates, miniature leaves, stems, and berry clusters appear, providing a visual map of how the vine will grow. The tiny blossoms (shown above on a Pinot Noir plant) emerge for only a few weeks—one of the most critical periods in a vineyard. Flowers turn into grapes only if pollinated. If the weather is warm and sunny at this time, bloom passes quickly and clusters become tightly packed with grapes. Rain and wind disrupt the self-pollination process, causing thinner fruit clusters.

TENDING THE VINES

As grapes proliferate and fatten in the summer, so do vine leaves. That makes for gorgeous, verdant landscapes, but too much greenery obstructs sun and wind. Pruning machines help vineyard workers manage canopy growth, hedging the tops of vines when they start to arc over the rows. Vineyard crews also remove leaves near fruit clusters by hand to allow light penetration. Exposure to sun is essential to ripening—increasing sugar levels to give grapes rich fruity flavor—and limiting some of the vegetal characteristics (green bean and bell pepper aromas) of grapes. Adequate airflow is also important, keeping fruit dry and free of fungal disease and preventing grapes from burning in hot, dry zones like Washington's Columbia Valley.

HARVEST: HURRY-UP TIME

Just like prolonged exposure to sun colors our skin, it darkens the skins of grapes, a process called veraison. White varietals change color first, with reds following a few weeks later. After veraison, a vine diverts its energy from leaves, shoots, and roots to the grapes; this is when grapes really begin their transformation to wine, acquiring distinctive varietal characteristics. Winemakers start sampling grapes in late summer, noting sweetness and maturity to determine the optimal time to harvest. Autumn is the most frenzied time in the vineyard; crews often begin picking before sunrise, and crush pads overflow with full grape bins. Grapes ripen according to type and location within the vineyard, but once they're ready—when sugar and acid strike an ideal balance—they need to be picked quickly. Ripe merlot grapes are pictured here, harvested in October amid turning leaves.

LET THE WINEMAKING BEGIN

After harvest, attention turns from vine to wine. Fruit from the field is de-stemmed and crushed, creating must, a composition of juice, pulp, seeds, and skins (depending on the type of wine). White wine grapes are crushed immediately, pressed off skins and seeds, and transferred to stainless steel fermentation tanks or to oak barrels. Red varietal grapes begin fermenting prior to pressing, which can be done in a traditional basket press like the one shown here. (Tinhorn Creek winemaker Sandra Oldfield is pictured above, assisting a member of her all-female production crew.) Next, juice is transferred to settling tanks, and in some cases, blending tanks, before aging in barrels or stainless tanks. Crushing and pressing methods, fermentation and aging timelines, and equipment vary widely from winery to winery, depending on a winemaker's philosophy and preferences.

36

KEEP IT CLEAN

Modest winemakers are fond of saying there's not that much to making wine, you've just got to keep it clean. A sanitary environment and airtight tanks go a long way toward keeping wine safe from taint and pathogens. This dual manhole tank allows production crew to thoroughly clear tanks of settled pomace. The dimpled surface on the tank is a cooling jacket, which permits precise temperature control, a key to slow, steady fermentation.

ANALYZE THIS

Winemakers frequently taste wines as they develop, but taste—even at an expert level—is subjective. Chemistry provides an objective assessment of wine and makes it possible to compare chemical differences that account for variation in flavor and alcohol content. Winemakers and lab staff draw samples to measure brix (sugar concentration), acid, tannins, sulfur dioxide, and alcohol, and perform additional chemical analysis throughout vinification. Every winery has a laboratory set-up of some sort; at smaller wineries, where space is precious, fairly rudimentary arrangements are often found in a winemaker's office.

THE BIG SLEEP

In the world of wine, barrels possess a romantic allure similar to that of cork: both are hewn from natural materials and vintners have used them for ages. While many winemakers now embrace screw-top seals, it's unlikely that anyone will abandon wooden barrels for alternative storage. Oak infuses wine with vanilla, butter, and spice flavors and, because the pores in the wood allow a small amount of air to seep in over time, wine oxidizes slowly, developing a mellow texture. During construction, barrels are held over small, wood-fueled fires to char their interiors to a light, medium or heavy toast. Winemakers select barrels of varying toasts depending on wine variety. French oak dominates the market, though barrels constructed from American and Hungarian oak are gaining acceptance.

THE MOMENT OF TRUTH

The ultimate test for wine is not in the vineyard or the lab, but in the glass sitting on the table in front of you. The strenuous process of coaxing a great wine from the earth comes to an end when it's bottled and shipped, transferred from the knowing hands of the winery to the consumer who simply wants something tasty to drink with dinner. Winemaker Dave Paige of Adelsheim Winery, pictured above in the barrel cellar, believes that the best wines satisfy both wine geeks and the rest of us. "A great wine is complex because it has to achieve balance of flavor, aroma, and texture. That gives the wine nerds something to talk about, but for those who aren't interested in all that, it's just a really yummy wine. You don't need to know why in order to enjoy it." Cheers to that. ❧

The Wineries

Oregon

In the 1990s, Oregon was associated with beer, not wine, earning a reputation as the epicenter of the craft brewing movement. Now it can add craft winemaking to its résumé. The number of wineries in Oregon doubled between 1995 and 2005, and today the state boasts more than 305. But that figure tells only part of the story. The Oregon Wine Board estimates that more than four hundred brands exist, including winemakers' second labels, joint projects, and boutique wines produced by artisans who effectively squat, or rent use of facilities, at larger wineries.

This phenomenon spawned events such as the Indie Wine Festival, an annual showcase of wines produced in small lots that rarely make it to market. It's a logical evolution of an industry founded by iconoclasts, and the diversity of entrants—including Syrah, Sangiovese, and Muscat—demonstrates that Oregon winemakers have moved beyond Pinot Noir. Though Pinot Noir represents the lion's share of grapes grown and wine produced here, winemakers in southern Oregon are staking a claim to warm-weather varietals. So don't be surprised when you spot a bottle of Oregon Zinfandel. ⁊

THE WINERIES

Abacela Vineyards & Winery

Adelsheim Vineyard

Archery Summit Winery

Argyle Winery

Bethel Heights Vineyard

Brandborg Vineyard & Winery

The Carlton Winemakers Studio

Del Rio Vineyards & Winery

Domaine Drouhin Oregon

Erath Vineyards

King Estate Winery

Sokol Blosser Winery

Valley View Winery

Willamette Valley Vineyards

People start wineries for all sorts of reasons—vocation, retirement, vanity—but there can't be too many who cite food allergies as a motivating factor. Earl Jones, a physician who founded Abacela Winery with his wife, Hilda, in 1995, is allergic to garlic and onions (poor soul!), so he relies on chiles and peppers to enliven his food. After he developed a taste for wine while living in San Francisco from 1964 to 1973, he began searching for a wine that could stand up to the spicy foods he loves. He found it in Tempranillo, a robust, inky red with all the brio of a flamenco dancer. When Earl decided to switch gears from immunology to enology, cultivating Tempranillo became his raison d'être.

A science junkie, Earl loves to experiment. When Hilda vetoed his plan to plant their initial twelve-acre plot solely with Tempranillo vines, he decided to test the limits of soil and climate, sowing eighteen varietals to determine which thrived and which flopped. Tempranillo is still Abacela's hallmark, but the winery also turns out captivating Malbec, Syrah, and Viognier, plus limited bottlings of port, Albariño, and Blanco Dulce, a powerful white dessert wine.

Earl and winemaker Kiley Evans continue to experiment with Tempranillo clones, widening their toolkit of flavors and textures when blending grapes from various slopes and vines. "There's not a lot of interest in Spanish cultivars here, so they're difficult to obtain," Evans says with a tinge of frustration. "UC Davis had a few, but they were used to make hearty Burgundy-style jug wines in California." While early California Tempranillo was a flavor bomb used to beef up cheap wines, Earl was betting on the varietal's response to rich soil, higher elevation, and less intense heat—the conditions found in Roseburg.

In the beginning, Abacela, a short country drive from Roseburg's center, attracted serious wine hounds from San Francisco, Portland, and Seattle. "We had a buzzer system, so if I was out on a tractor, I'd know when guests arrived. Our average sale was a little less than two cases per customer, and they would go back home and tell their friends about us. With a different varietal, we wouldn't have had that instant clientele, but Tempranillo was so unusual that word of mouth spread like wildfire."

Interest in Tempranillo grew as Americans became more familiar with Spanish cuisine and wines, which have generated fervent interest in recent years thanks to innovative chefs such as Ferrán Adriá and Juan Mari Arzak. Foodies who fall in love with lush Riojas are eager to try New World Tempranillo, and this has helped Abacela. The winery still draws visitors curious to try the varietal; only now it's often not their first sip of the stuff.

It's a fun place to visit, exuding a relaxed vibe that invites questions and easy conversation. Situated on five hundred acres, Abacela features three distinctive plots among its Fault Line Vineyards, creating a gorgeous patchwork of vines. When the leaves turn in autumn, the division between varietals is blatant: Tempranillo darkens to deep crimson, Syrah becomes variegated, and Viognier remains a vivid green.

Abacela's winemaking philosophy is to let the grapes do as much of the work as possible, keeping human intervention to a minimum. Most contemporary winemakers believe that great wine depends mostly on how fruit is treated in the vineyard, contending that you can't transform mediocre grapes into outstanding vino. Conversely, if you start with well-managed fruit, you're well on your way to bottling a delicious elixir.

To that end, the hilltop winery features gravity-flow production, a macerating method regarded as the gentlest method for extracting juice from grapes. On a tour of the facility, visitors can witness an escalator conveying fruit to the top of a hopper. You'll also see the fermentation room, crammed with small-batch bins that require manual punch-downs twice daily to control the temperature and formation of carbon dioxide. A clipboard containing careful notations hangs from each bin, testament to Abacela's hands-on approach.

Back in the cozy, cavelike tasting room, no bigger than a foyer, you can munch on salty crackers and compare Tempranillo vintages. There's a window into the full-to-bursting barrel room, where you might see Evans and his assistants extracting ribbons of wine from barrels with an elegant glass wine thief. Pourers are eager to discuss the differences among varietals and talk about Abacela's unique vineyards. (Abacela currently cultivates about 80 percent of its grapes, buying the rest from other Umpqua Valley growers.)

In fine weather, guests can picnic by a cannon the Joneses bought at auction in Pennsylvania. It's not just for show: to celebrate the winery's tenth anniversary, in 2005, the Joneses fired off ten shots, appropriately marking their success in introducing an obscure varietal to American imbibers with a very loud bang. ⁀

44

ABACELA VINEYARDS & WINERY // 12500 Lookingglass Road, Roseburg, OR 97470

T 541.679.6642
F 541.679.4455
E wine@abacela.com

www.abacela.com

ACCESS
Eleven miles from Roseburg. From Interstate 5 southbound, take exit 119. Follow Highway 99 for 3 miles to Route 42, and turn right. Proceed 1.5 miles, and turn left on Brockway Road. Head north a short distance, turning left onto Lookingglass Road. The winery will be on your left. From Interstate 5 northbound, take exit 113. Travel west on Clark's Branch Road, then north on Highway 99 to Dillard. Take a left on Brockway Road, and another left onto Lookingglass Road. The winery will be on your left.

Hours open for visits and tasting:
11AM–5PM daily, except major holidays.

TASTINGS & TOURS
$2 per taste for Abacela's reserve wines; all others complimentary.

Tours: 1 and 3PM daily. Appointment necessary.

Typical wines offered: Tempranillo, Syrah, Merlot, Claret, Malbec, and Viognier. Limited productions of Cabernet Franc, Dolcetto, Grenache, Nebbiolo, Albariño, Graciano, and port.

Sales of wine-related items: logo wineglasses only.

PICNICS & PROGRAMS
Picnic area open to the public. No picnic ingredients sold in tasting room.

Special events: Spring Umpqua Valley Barrel Tour in late April or early May.

Wine club.

RIBERO DEL DUERO 5,546MI

MENDOZA 6,290MI

BORDEAUX 5,429MI

Abacela↓

ROSEBURG 11MI

Adelsheim Vineyard

OWNERS: DAVID & GINNY ADELSHEIM, JACK & LYNN LOACKER // WINEMAKER: DAVE PAIGE

David Adelsheim describes his winery's Pinot Noirs as rich and silky, wines that don't put drinkers off with monolithic structure when young. "We're focused on making Pinots that are really delicious, and our concept of what's delicious doesn't include bitter tannins." But Adelsheim admits that it took some time—like a couple of decades—to really hit the groove. "There's a huge swath of Pinot styles, and we were confused for a while. Then we said, 'We're just going to make the Pinots we love to drink.'"

That confusion was not due to flaws or problems particular to Adelsheim Vineyard. The fact is, Oregon Pinot Noir vintners have endured some serious trial and error in the process of cultivating their chosen grape. The story of Adelsheim Vineyard, established in 1971, is emblematic of the evolution of the Willamette Valley wine industry as a whole.

Founders David and Ginny Adelsheim began without a blueprint. Like many baby boomers, they became acquainted with the pleasures of food and wine while traveling around Europe. David returned home and read every wine book he could find. He started to think it might be possible to raise grapes in the Willamette Valley, despite expert opinions to the contrary. In 1971, the Adelsheims bought nineteen poppy-strewn acres in the picturesque Chehalem Hills and started sowing Pinot Noir, as well as Pinot Gris, Riesling, and Chardonnay.

"You have to adopt a 1971 mind-set to understand why we got into this. People were leaving other professions and going to farms—it was a romantic vision and a lifestyle choice," Adelsheim recalls. "It allowed us to create something from the ground up and sell directly to consumers in a way that wasn't really available at the time."

Adelsheim and other Willamette Valley trailblazers spent the 1970s planting, replanting, and experimenting with various clones—generally learning how to grow grapes. In 1978, he made his first vintage in the basement of his home at the original Quarter Mile Vineyard plot. The 1980s saw significant growth and investment in Yamhill County. Key blind tastings around the country and in France showed that Oregon was capable of producing world-class Pinot Noir. In 1987, revered Burgundy *négociant* Robert Drouhin bought 225 acres in the Dundee Hills. He and daughter Véronique, who would become winemaker of Domaine Drouhin Oregon, were confident that this was the best place in America to grow the exalted grape of Burgundy—Pinot Noir. The Drouhin venture sent a message to the wine world that Oregon was to be taken seriously. It was a shot in the arm for Adelsheim and other Willamette Valley winemakers.

Adelsheim considers the 1990s the turning point for Oregon Pinot Noir. Instead of comparing their handiwork to the wines of Burgundy, winemakers turned inward and sought to craft Pinot Noir expressive of its origin, the climatic and topographic qualities unique to Oregon. "People were saying, okay, what sets our wine apart from other regions? Elements of fresh fruit and enough acidity to provide backbone distinguish us from California, where acidity doesn't play as much, and from Burgundy, which has less pronounced fruit." Continued experimentation in the vineyard and an emphasis on intentional crop management contributed to more intensely concentrated grapes and richer, fuller wines. A great 1998 vintage kicked off a half-decade of consistent vintages, converting more wine lovers to Pinot Noir.

ADELSHEIM VINEYARD // 16800 N.E. Calkins Lane, Newberg, OR 97132

T 503.538.3652
F 503.538.2248
E info@adelsheim.com

www.adelsheimvineyard.com

ACCESS
About 45 minutes from Portland. From Portland, take Interstate 5 south to exit 294. Turn right onto Highway 99W. Go about 17 miles through Tigard, Sherwood, and Newberg. Turn right onto Highway 240 and follow it as it curves left out of Newberg for 1.5 miles until you reach Tangen Road. Turn right and follow Tangen Road for 1 mile. Turn left on N. Valley Road and proceed about 2 miles to Calkins Lane. Turn right and go half a mile until you reach the far end of a white fence running along the right side of the road. Turn right at the gates; the winery's main parking lot and entrance are to the left.

Hours open for visits and tasting:
11AM–4PM daily, Memorial Day through September and December 26–31;
11AM–4PM Wednesday–Sunday, October to Memorial Day.

TASTINGS & TOURS
$10 to taste five to six current releases.

Tours: Usually at 11AM daily; $20. Appointment necessary.

Typical wines offered: Pinot Noir, Pinot Gris, Chardonnay, Pinot Blanc, Pinot Auxerrois, TF (Tocai Friulano), and Deglacé (ice wine).

Sales of wine-related items.

PICNICS & PROGRAMS
Picnic area open to the public. No picnic ingredients sold in tasting room.

Special events: Memorial Weekend Open House; Thanksgiving in Wine Country; wine club events.

Wine club.

The late '90s also marked the rebirth of Adelsheim Vineyard. Creative, energetic young staffers infused the winery with new blood. Partners came on, providing financial stability that allowed the winery to expand. A sturdy new facility incorporating a gravity-flow winery, offices, and event space was built between 1993 and 1997 at one of Adelsheim's several vineyard sites.

It's taken another ten years for Adelsheim to construct a proper tasting room. No one thought that tourists would venture onto little-traveled country roads to visit a winery. But people kept showing up, and the dining room that was also used for meetings and events did double duty to accommodate wine country ramblers. In 2005, tasting-room proceedings were moved to the crush area of the winery; plans to remodel the tasting room and office space are under way.

But Adelsheim hasn't needed a showy tasting room to attract or win over fans. The winery has a compelling story—and the wines to back it up. Winemaker Dave Paige joined the team in 2001, and his thoughtful approach and dedication cemented Adelsheim's reputation for supple, lovingly crafted wines. He is fascinated by the complexity of Pinot Noir, referring to it as a variety that never ceases to be puzzling. "You can make a Pinot Noir and say, Yeah, this tastes great... but I wonder what I could do differently next time?"

Paige's attitude fairly sums up Adelsheim Vineyard's journey. It knows what it does well but is never satisfied with the status quo, regarding curiosity as an essential ingredient of mastery. ❧

Archery Summit Winery

OWNER: PINE RIDGE WINERY, LLC // WINEMAKER: ANNA MATZINGER

If a love of Pinot Noir draws you to the Willamette Valley, Archery Summit is one winery you should not overlook. Like boutique producers in rainy Yamhill County, Archery Summit focuses solely on handcrafted Pinot Noir, turning out exemplary single-origin wines. Unlike some of its brethren that don't have the resources to accommodate a steady stream of tourists, Archery Summit is well funded (Napa Valley's Pine Ridge Winery is the parent company) and designed to educate and entertain visitors.

Tastings and tours carry fees and must be arranged in advance, but planning a stop at Archery Summit is worth the effort and expense. For starters, tours offer ample opportunity to sample the grape, including sips of variously aged Pinots pulled from barrels in Archery Summit's basalt-rock cave. Then there's the view, a gorgeous valley vista encircled by the Dundee Hills, allowing glimpses of Mounts Hood and Jefferson on clear days and evoking the misty English countryside when gray clouds dominate the sky.

Situated amid one of four densely planted estate vineyards, the sand-colored chateau is much larger than it first appears. Tours commence in a tasting room no bigger than an apartment kitchen, surprisingly small given the grandeur of the winery. Archery Summit, which reaped its first harvest in 1993 and now produces between ten thousand and twelve thousand cases annually, didn't quite anticipate the recent spike in Pinot Noir interest. But as the moody, food-friendly varietal receives more exposure, increasing numbers of Pinotphiles want to visit the region in which the temperamental grape thrives. In 2005, Archery Summit was astounded to see its wine club jump to 2,600 members, up from 1,400 the year before.

Rather than saving wine for your visit's conclusion, Archery Summit kicks off tours by pouring generous glasses of Premier Cuvée Pinot Noir for guests to enjoy while they walk around. Crafted as a singular expression of the vintage, it is the only Archery Summit wine blended with fruit from each of its vineyards; the others are single-vineyard Pinots. This moderately priced wine, the most accessible of Archery Summit's lineup, accounts for 70 percent of the winery's output.

Carved out of a rocky incline, Archery Summit was designed specifically for Pinot Noir production, a fact that distinguishes it from wineries that make a host of varietals. The hillside site facilitated a six-level gravity-feed system, a gentle winemaking process that allows grape matter to flow naturally downhill on its journey from whole fruit to fermented juice, precluding the need for pressing and pumping. Relying on gravity instead of forceful treatment helps preserve the pure fruit flavor of delicate Pinot Noir, a thin-skinned grape that will bruise easily.

Tours mimic this journey, climbing to the top floor of the winery, where grape clusters are sorted by hand and emptied into the de-stemmer. The fruit slides down a chute into a stainless steel tank for cold soaking, which extracts color and flavor from grapes prior to fermentation. Winemaker Anna Matzinger has been experimenting with wooden fermentation tanks, tapered vats that require a fair amount of babying and look quaint and rustic alongside sleek stainless steel towers. Matzinger says it's difficult to quantify the effect of fermenting Pinot Noir in oak but believes the primary difference is in the resulting mouthfeel. "Stainless steel imparts a more homogenous impression in terms of structure, while wood tanks contribute a heterogeneous impression—more depth." Matzinger also ferments some fruit as whole clusters, retaining stem material to lend flavor intensity and a hint of allspice.

After fermentation, wine cascades into settling tanks before traveling through hoses, again by gravity, into French oak barrels, which are then carried into the cave for aging. And what a cave! Archery Summit bored straight into the slope to sculpt a subterranean cave, the only one of its kind in Oregon. This was done in part for aesthetic reasons—and it is undeniably cool, the bumpy surface rock covered with a thin layer of spray-on concrete—but also for optimal barrel aging. The cave naturally maintains a temperature between 57 and 60 degrees Fahrenheit year-round and subtly slants downhill, sticking with the gravity theme. It terminates in a Gothic tasting room used for the barrel-tasting portion of the tour and for special events.

Matzinger asserts that the wine is most fragile once barrel aging is complete. "Gravity matters most at the end of the process, once the wine's matrix is formed." The production team uses inert gas to siphon wine into blending tanks situated two stories below the cave. Then the liquid descends another level to a bottling tank, which is fitted onto a mechanical lift. Now the wine is ready to be bottled: a pulley system raises the lift thirty-six feet upward to meet the bottling line, cleverly circumventing any need for pumps.

These steps may seem unnecessarily painstaking, and, to be sure, fantastic Pinot Noir can be achieved by other winemaking methods. But the smoothness and sophistication of Archery Summit's Pinot are apparent at first sip: these are thrilling wines. And the winery is an outstanding example of gravity-feed craftsmanship, plainly illustrating how the system works. That alone is worth the price of admission. ∾

ARCHERY SUMMIT WINERY // 18599 N.E. Archery Summit Road, Dayton, OR 97114

T 503.864.4300
F 503.864.4038
E aswconcierge@archerysummit.com

www.archerysummit.com

ACCESS
About a 45-minute drive from Portland. From Interstate 5 southbound, take exit 294 toward Highway 99W. Continue on 99W through Tigard, Sherwood, Newberg, and Dundee. Approximately 1 mile south of Dundee, turn right onto Archery Summit Road. Follow this gravel road until you reach the winery's entrance gate.

Hours open for visits and tasting:
10AM–4:30PM daily, except major holidays.

TASTINGS & TOURS
$10 includes a flight of four wines, including single-vineyard Pinot Noirs.

Tours: 10:30AM and 1 and 3PM daily. $20 includes barrel sampling and tastes of single-vineyard Pinot Noirs. Appointment necessary.

Typical wines offered: Vineyard-designated Pinot Noirs.

Sales of wine-related items.

PICNICS & PROGRAMS
No picnic area open to the public.

Special events: Annual Memorial Weekend in Wine Country; Thanksgiving in Wine Country; Valentine's Day Open House; Dundee Hills Passport Tour in April; seasonal dinners and weekend events.

Wine club.

Argyle Winery co-owner and winemaker Rollin Soles never deviates from a single overarching mantra: make consistently high-quality wines. It's not enough to make a batch of outstanding wines one year, only to deliver a disappointing product the following year. Soles believes consistency is essential to earning consumers' trust and critical acclaim—and he has the patience to defer immediate gratification and adhere to his code. As a producer of sparkling wines, he has no choice.

Sparkling wine presents a number of challenges that still wines do not. For starters, many think of it as a special-occasion beverage suitable only for toasts. Though wine aficionados exalt bubbly's knack for complementing almost any food, most people can't conceive of drinking it with a meal. When we do drink sparkling wine, it's often at a wedding or party, and it's usually of poor stock because hosts assume that guests will have only a sip or two anyway.

"Americans don't drink that much sparkling, and our knowledge of sparkling wines is limited by name recognition—Champagne," Soles says. "And there are some awful wines with that label." (True Champagne must hail from the chalky soils of France's most northerly wine region, Champagne, just a couple hours' drive east of Paris.) While superb Champagne, such as Bollinger or Dom Pérignon, may set the gold standard for bubbly, exceptional sparkling wine is made in Italy (Prosecco), Spain (Cava), Australia, Argentina, France's Loire Valley, and North America.

In 1979, while enrolled in the master of enology program at UC Davis, Soles, a Texas native, visited Oregon's Willamette Valley and fell in love with the landscape and climate. More important, he recognized the valley's suitability to growing the grapes traditionally used to make sparkling wine: Chardonnay and Pinot Noir. "The American thing to do would be to dive right into the business, but I needed experience," Soles says. With his heart set on Oregon, he began his winemaking career in California and then moved to Australia, where he sharpened his craft at Brian Croser's Petaluma Winery. Croser provided the financial backing to found Argyle, and in 1987, Soles returned to Oregon.

Cringeworthy associations with cheap wedding bubbly aside, capital and the difficult, time-consuming production of sparkling wine are the hurdles that prevent more winemakers from making the stuff. "Sparkling wine is very expensive to produce," Soles says. "I had to grow, make, and bottle four vintages before I made my first sale." Sparkling wine must age longer than still wine, requiring wineries to fund operations for years before the product is ready for market. And transforming grape juice into bubbly is more complicated than making red or white wine, requiring a tricky series of chemical reactions that renders the liquid vulnerable to contamination and presents many opportunities for error. "You're blending Pinot Noir and Chardonnay. There's no other beverage that combines such disparate liquids."

Because only a tiny portion of the grape is used for sparkling wines, the fruit must be first-rate. "When you make red wine, you use the entire grape—seeds, pulp, skins—so you extract a lot of flavor. For whites, you're not using the seeds or skins, but you have the entire pulp. With sparkling, there are no skins or seeds, only the pulp from the heart of the berry. You don't have any of the pulp that was next to the skin, which holds a lot of flavor. . . . So the fruit has to be damn good to start with."

Argyle's upbeat staff is well versed in the quirks of making bubbly. The winery, housed in an old hazelnut-drying facility, doesn't offer tours, but you can gain quite an education in the tasting room. The remodeled Victorian house was Dundee's city hall before Argyle acquired the building; today it is one of the most elegant tasting rooms in Oregon, with a lush, vibrant garden of native plants to match. When it opened to visitors in 1991, there was little tourist traffic in Dundee, and Oregon was slumped in a recession. But Argyle knew it was important to have a public face and to tell people about its wines.

Now Argyle is a well-known destination and the winery sells everything it makes, parceling out its forty-thousand- to fifty-thousand-case production on an allocation basis. Argyle's sparklers include brut, blanc

---

50

ARGYLE WINERY // 691 Highway 99W, P.O. Box 290, Dundee, OR 97115

T 888.427.4953; 503.538.8520
F 503.538.2055
E tastingroom@argylewinery.com

www.argylewinery.com

ACCESS
About 45 minutes from Portland. From Portland, take Interstate 5 south to exit 294. Turn right onto Highway 99W and follow it through Newberg to Dundee. The winery is on the left in downtown Dundee.

Hours open for visits and tasting: 11AM–5PM daily, except major holidays.

TASTINGS & TOURS
Bubbly flight includes four wines for $5; Red, White, and Bubbly flight includes five wines for $7; individual tastes are $1.50.

Tours: No tours.

Typical wines offered: Brut, blanc de blancs, brut rosé, Chardonnay, Riesling, Pinot Noir, and Merlot.

Sales of wine-related items.

PICNICS & PROGRAMS
Picnic area open to the public on the patio and in the garden. No picnic ingredients sold in tasting room.

Special events: Dundee Hills Passport Tour in April; Memorial Weekend Open House; Thanksgiving in Wine Country.

Wine club.

de blancs (made only with Chardonnay grapes), and brut rosé, and it also produces Riesling, Chardonnay, and several Pinot Noirs. Its Spirithouse Pinot Noir honors the pioneer woman who occupied the farmhouse long before it was a tasting room and whose ghostly presence is rumored to remain there. Another resident you may encounter is Snowball, the winery cat.

As more money flows into the Willamette Valley, it's likely that entrepreneurs will invest in sparkling wine. Argyle has paved the way for future success, and also has set an estimable benchmark. ❧

Bethel Heights Vineyard

OWNERS: TED CASTEEL, TERRY CASTEEL, PAT DUDLEY, BARBARA DUDLEY & MARILYN WEBB
WINEMAKER: TERRY CASTEEL

Sometimes a magazine article can change your life. Bethel Heights Vineyard manager Ted Casteel read an article in *The New Yorker* in the 1970s about a professor who quit teaching to grow potatoes. "The gist of it was: If you're going to do something, do what you love." A simple message, to be sure, but one that is particularly resonant if you happen to be pondering a career change.

At the time, Ted and his wife, Pat Dudley, were professors of European history in Michigan. Ted's twin brother, Terry, had just completed his training to become a licensed psychologist and was living in Seattle with his wife, Marilyn Webb, who worked at the University of Washington. All were academics who were unconvinced that academia was the life for them. Living thousands of miles apart, the two couples grew interested in wine and the pleasures of the table, perusing bottle shops and staging get-togethers with friends to learn about and try different wines. "Twins have a way of knowing what the other is doing," Marilyn observes. During family vacations, wine was central to conversations, and blind tastings were common. "It was a revolutionary time, and people were making lifestyle changes," she remembers. "For us, growing grapes was a way to bring work life and home life together, which was very attractive."

The two couples began scouting vineyard sites in 1977 and fell in love with a property in the Eola Hills. The rural area is just a short distance from Salem, but it feels a world apart from the mundane capital. From Bethel Heights, you can drive miles in any direction and see nothing but vineyards, country farms, and the occasional hawk. Unmarred but slightly more populous today, the area must have felt positively remote thirty years ago. When the Casteel contingent bought the land, thirteen acres were newly planted with Chenin Blanc, Riesling, and Gewürztraminer; the owner was forced to sell because he had promised his investors too-quick returns. Spring-fed, undulating, and cooled by the windy Van Duzer corridor, it appeared to be a prime growing location. And the sunsets weren't too shabby, either.

Just starting out, the whole group worked in the vineyard, clearing, planting, and replanting. They built their homes on the land and divvied up labor, including child-care duty. Bethel Heights established its reputation as a prized vineyard, supplying fruit to Domaine Drouhin Oregon, Adelsheim Vineyard, Rex Hill, and Santa Cruz's Bonny Doon Vineyard. Starting a winery was the logical next step. Around this time, each person slipped into the role that played to his or her strengths. Terry Casteel dove into winemaking, taking classes at UC Davis and apprenticing at Sokol Blosser Winery, while Ted tended the vineyards. Pat and Marilyn spearheaded sales and marketing efforts. (Pat's sister Barbara Dudley was an original Bethel Heights investor, but she remained on the East Coast until moving to Portland in 1999. She currently chairs the winery's board of directors.)

Since establishing the winery in 1984, Bethel Heights has concentrated on producing Pinot Noir. Thirty-seven of the fifty acres composing the estate vineyard are planted with Pinot Noir clones; the remaining acreage yields Chardonnay, Pinot Gris, and Pinot Blanc. Situated south of the Red Hills of Dundee—Oregon's primary Pinot region—the Eola Hills have shallow soils and a pronounced cooling effect from the Van Duzer corridor. Ted Casteel says these conditions lend Pinot Noir black fruit aromas, spicy flavor, and bright acidity. "Pinot Noir is a creature of place. Terry refers to it as catlike in that way."

Though they could afford only a modest tasting room, the Bethel Heights gang knew that it could become a significant part of their business. "From the beginning, about 25 percent of our income came from the tasting room. That's your dream because [visitors] become your friends and you're selling wine at retail," Marilyn says. But by 1999, it was time for an upgrade. Bethel Heights contracted to build a new production facility and tasting room on a portion of land the owners had saved expressly for the purpose. The south-facing room and patio grant spectacular views, with the better part of two walls given over to windows. With a kitchen behind the tasting counter and a large communal table bathed in light, it feels like someone's very nice home—and guests are usually in no hurry to leave.

Family members also tend to linger. Though he didn't anticipate getting into the wine business, Terry and Marilyn's eldest son, Ben, now works alongside his dad as assistant winemaker. Younger brother John works in the cellar at Rex Hill Vineyards in Newberg. Ted and Pat's daughters, Jesse and Mimi, help manage publicity and sales, and it's likely that Mimi will inherit viticultural duties from her father. Both generations appear surprised and delighted to be working together. "We've all found a place for ourselves," Marilyn says. "Like the Gallos, we've survived because each person is in charge of a different area." ❧

BETHEL HEIGHTS VINEYARD // 6060 Bethel Heights Road N.W., Salem, OR 97304

T 503.581.2262
F 503.581.0943
E info@bethelheights.com

www.bethelheights.com

ACCESS
About 1 hour from Portland. From Portland, take Interstate 5 south to the Salem Parkway exit. Stay on the Salem Parkway, which becomes Commercial Street, through town, about 5 miles. Stay in the center-right lane and turn right onto the Marion Street Bridge into West Salem. Follow signs to Wallace Road (Highway 221), go almost 6 miles on Wallace Road, and turn left on Zena Road. Continue about 4 miles and turn right on Bethel Heights Road N.W. Follow one-quarter mile to the winery.

Hours open for visits and tasting:
11AM–5PM Tuesday–Sunday, June–August;
11AM–5PM Saturday–Sunday, September–November and March–May. Closed December–February, except by appointment, and major holidays.

TASTINGS & TOURS
No charge for tasting.

Tours: Appointment recommended.

Typical wines offered: Pinot Noir, Pinot Gris, Pinot Blanc, and Chardonnay.

Sales of wine-related items.

PICNICS & PROGRAMS
Picnic area open to the public on the deck.
No picnic ingredients sold in tasting room.

Special events: Memorial Weekend Open House; Thanksgiving in Wine Country.

Wine club.

Brandborg Vineyard & Winery

OWNERS: **TERRY & SUE BRANDBORG** // WINEMAKER: **TERRY BRANDBORG**

This is one winery where you are guaranteed a great deal of personal attention—if not from one of the owners, then from the dedicated tasting-room staffers, all two of them. That's just the way things go in villages, where time passes slowly and the post office is still the best place to catch up on gossip.

Situated in Elkton, a hamlet halfway between the Oregon coast and the Interstate 5 corridor, Brandborg Winery has become a social hub for residents who were initially skeptical of California transplants Terry and Sue Brandborg. Today, the one-stoplight town, with a population hovering around 150, supports a handful of small, quality-focused wineries. A blip on the road for passersby en route to the Oregon Dunes or Coos Bay, Elkton is starting to see increased traffic from both touring oenophiles and winemakers in search of cheap enriched vineyard land. Terry Brandborg, a self-taught home winemaker from the Bay Area, was drawn to the Umpqua Valley upon realizing that he just couldn't afford to start a commercial winery in his home state. Once he studied the soil compositions and climatic conditions of the Umpqua, he was sold.

Located at the nexus of three mountain ranges, the Umpqua boasts unusual soil diversity and gets hit with maritime fog in the morning and breezes at the end of the day, all of which benefit finicky grapes such as Pinot Noir. Earl Jones, founder of Abacela Winery in nearby Roseburg, encouraged the Brandborgs to investigate Elkton, where growers have been cultivating Pinot Noir,

Brandborg's signature varietal, since 1972. Terry and Sue lucked into a 145-acre parcel of red-dirt land six miles outside of town, complete with exposed slopes and a comfortable farmhouse. Though they had plenty of land on which to construct a winery, the Brandborgs wanted to build an accessible facility where visitors could sample wine and view production without veering off the main drag.

For the winery, they chose a lot in what could be described as the center of town, poured the foundation in July 2002, and finished construction on September 30, just in time to crush fruit that started coming in the next day. Miraculously, the tasting room was ready in time to greet guests for Oregon's big Thanksgiving wine weekend. Constructed with a modest western-style front and built tall to accommodate the barrels in back, the laid-back tasting room is airy and big enough to host the large audiences that congregate year-round for live music shows.

In just a few years, Brandborg made a fine name for itself in a crowded local Pinot market, drawing more and more visitors and generating buzz at winemakers' dinners and regional wine shops. Though the wines speak for themselves, the Brandborgs' story—a mix of perseverance and serendipity—bears repeating.

Terry started making wine in San Francisco one afternoon in 1975 when his uncle invited him out to an Italian friend's suburban vineyard. "We picked some grapes, stomped them in the driveway with my hippie

friends, and breathed in that hot, hedonistic aroma." Terry's first batch of whiskey-barrel wine turned out well, and he joined a home winemakers' group and started lending a hand at a Mendocino vineyard in exchange for grapes. Before long, he set up a rudimentary basement facility and was producing five hundred cases of Pinot Noir, Chardonnay, and Riesling a year. All the while, he worked as a longshoreman, pulling 7AM-to-3PM shifts so he could peddle his wine to restaurants in the afternoon. Restaurateurs were impressed, and his wine popped up at trailblazing eateries like Bay Wolf and Chez Panisse. Eventually, Terry moved operations into rented warehouse space in a rough part of Richmond—far from the idyllic rolling hills often associated with wineries—and increased production to twenty-five hundred cases.

Terry longed for the countryside and a farmer's way of life, and when he met Sue at a wine tasting in Jackson Hole, Wyoming, in 1998, that dream started coming into focus. Sue worked in the medical field and didn't drink much wine (though a doctor had previously introduced her to Brandborg Pinot Noir, which she liked so much she went out and bought another bottle the same night), but she was eager to learn. Now Sue helps manage the winery and spends much of her time in the vineyard, scaring away greedy crows with shotgun blasts when necessary.

Starting out with five planted acres, the Brandborgs hope one day to cultivate fifty acres, growing enough grapes to become an estate winery. While the vines mature, Brandborg fulfills its annual output of eight thousand to ten thousand cases with fruit from other growers in the Umpqua Valley. Terry utilizes every square inch of space at the winery, stacking barrels five high. He employs time-intensive methods, using old basket presses to avoid the harsh tannins caused by ground-up grape seeds, and wooden punch-down fermentation containers he built in California.

As Brandborg wines have gained currency around Oregon and beyond, the winery has become more at home in its small-town community. Frequent concerts provide an opportunity for locals to socialize and get to know Brandborg wines—in a venue far more interesting than the Elkton post office. ☙

54

BRANDBORG VINEYARD & WINERY // 345 First Street, P.O. Box 506, Elkton, OR 97436

T 541.584.2870
F 541.584.2871
E info@brandborgwine.com

www.brandborgwine.com

ACCESS
From Interstate 5 southbound, take exit 162. Follow Route 38 about 20 miles west to Elkton. From Interstate 5 northbound, take exit 136. Follow Route 138 about 25 miles west to Elkton. The winery is the second building on the right as you enter town.

Hours open for visits and tasting:
11AM–5PM daily, except major holidays.

TASTINGS & TOURS
In summer months, $5 for tasting, refundable with a purchase of six or more bottles. No charge in winter months.

Tours: Informal guided tours of the production facility. Appointment necessary.

Typical wines offered: Pinot Noir, Pinot Gris, Chardonnay, Gewürztraminer, Riesling, Syrah, Cabernet Franc, and Scarlet Cuvée (Pinot Noir Rosé).

Sales of wine-related items.

PICNICS & PROGRAMS
Picnic area open to the public on the patio. Picnic ingredients sold in tasting room. Deli items available in summer months.

Special events: Spring Umpqua Valley Barrel Tour in late April or early May; live music in the tasting room frequently throughout the year.

Wine club.

The Carlton Winemakers Studio

OWNERS: ERIC HAMACHER, LUISA PONZI, AND NED & KIRSTEN LUMPKIN
WINEMAKERS: MULTIPLE INDEPENDENT WINEMAKERS UNDER ONE ROOF

The Carlton Winemakers Studio embodies an idea whose time has come. One winery with shared equipment, office space, and marketing efforts. Up to ten independent winemakers. Myriad superlative wines.

The greatest barrier between a budding winemaker and a fantastic bottle of wine is money: winemaking gear doesn't come cheap, and wine-country real estate is increasingly expensive, no matter the region. But put that equipment under one roof and provide enough space for each vintner to do her thing, and winemakers suddenly have access to the resources they need. It's a bit like a cooperative, except that the winemakers are tenants, not part owners. Besides its obvious benefits to winemakers, this concept is a boon to tourists, who are able to sample a revolving throng of wines at a single tasting room.

Eric Hamacher conceived of the Winemakers Studio after several years of crafting wines for his personal label while working at various Willamette Valley wineries. It was a gypsylike approach: by renting space and equipment at the wineries, he could afford to establish Hamacher Wines, which earned consistent raves. But Hamacher was unable to leverage the wineries for marketing purposes, and he always got last dibs on machinery. Fighting to keep his label going, Hamacher came up with an egalitarian model to help fellow winemakers who, like him, were interested in making around two thousand cases a year but found the cost of founding a full-scale winery prohibitive.

Hamacher and his wife, Luisa Ponzi—second-generation winemaker at the esteemed Ponzi Vineyards in Beaverton—partnered with Ned and Kirsten Lumpkin to make the studio a reality. The Lumpkins had recently retired from their Seattle construction business, known for its innovative eco-friendly buildings, and invested in the thirty-three-acre Lazy River vineyard in Yamhill County. They needed a winemaker, and Hamacher needed backing to fund his own winery. It was a fortuitous union that led to the creation of the Carlton Winemakers Studio as well as the Lazy River label.

In March 2001, the partners broke ground on a rural patch of land just removed from downtown Carlton, a tiny enclave with preserved Main Street allure, a couple of notable restaurants, and a roster of top-notch artisan winemakers. Much smaller and farther off the beaten path than nearby Yamhill County winery hubs Newberg, Dundee, and McMinnville, Carlton is a wine country gem on the rise. The Winemakers Studio could be considered its star attraction. It is a striking building, calling to mind a contemporary barn with unexpected angles and lots of windows. All construction materials were sourced within a two-hundred-mile radius of Carlton, many of them reused. A hefty sliding door leading to the tasting room was made with wood from school gymnasium bleachers; steel beams came from a former Wal-Mart store.

Energy efficiency was the guiding design principle. Huge, strategically placed windows mean lights rarely need to be on, and the entire space is highly functional, though its footprint is small. Most features were engineered to serve multiple purposes—the production area even includes a rock-climbing wall where various hoses are stored. (Hamacher is an avid climber and figures that the wall provides good workplace stress relief.)

The winery is just big enough for ten winemakers to work side by side, producing a maximum of 17,500 cases annually. During harvest, winemakers must work

---

THE CARLTON WINEMAKERS STUDIO // 801 N. Scott Street, P.O. Box 279, Carlton, OR 97111

T 503.852.6100
F 503.852.9519
E info@winemakersstudio.com

www.winemakersstudio.com

ACCESS
About 45 minutes from Portland. Take Interstate 5 south to exit 289 toward Tualatin/Sherwood. Head west on S.W. Nyberg Road. Take a slight left onto S.W. Tualatin-Sherwood Road and continue 4.5 miles. Turn left onto S.W. Pacific Highway/Highway 99W and continue 8.5 miles. Turn right onto Highway 240 and continue 6 miles. Take a slight left onto N.E. Kuehne Road, which becomes N.E. Hendricks Road and then E. Main Street. Follow Main Street through the first blinking light in Carlton and turn right onto N. Yamhill/Route 47. Turn left onto Lincoln Road.

Hours open for visits and tasting:
11AM–5PM daily, February–December.

TASTINGS & TOURS
Complimentary tastes of Carlton Winemakers Studio label wines; featured flights $8–$12; individual pours $3–$5.

Tours: Informal guided tours of the production facility. Appointment necessary.

Typical wines offered: Wide selection of wines; varies depending on winemakers in residence.

Sales of wine-related items.

PICNICS & PROGRAMS
No picnic area open to the public. Light menu served on premises. Selection of cheeses, charcuterie, crackers, and espresso served year-round; tapas menu also available in summer.

Special events: Wednesday Night Dinners, including chef-winemaker's dinners the first Wednesday of the month; seasonal wine education seminars; Memorial Weekend Open House; Thanksgiving in Wine Country.

together to coordinate staggered grape deliveries and use of the crush pad. A manic energy pervades the space, and cooperation is critical at a time when winemakers run on little sleep. But it's also a great way for vintners to learn from one another—and debate the best way to make wine—and check out fruit from a variety of vineyards.

The Studio's unique layout and emphasis on green solutions make for a highly informative tour, but the real action is in the tasting room and on the adjacent patio. Sunlight floods the simple, chic room by late morning, amplifying the gold and ruby hues of freshly poured glasses of wine. It is more like a wine bar than a tasting room, offering flights that change frequently to showcase the wide-ranging portfolios of very different winemakers. Espresso and a light menu are served, and the L-shaped counter and bistro tables contribute to the bar atmosphere.

Because the lineup of wines varies week to week, the Studio draws curious first-time visitors as well as repeat customers who, above all else, can count on outstanding wines. The Studio has been at capacity since it opened, and sometimes it has a waiting list. Some tenants, such as acclaimed indies Andrew Rich and Scott Paul, have been on board since day one, while others—including Lynn Penner-Ash and Tony Soter— went on to found eponymous wineries. The studio concept is a trend in the making; keep your eye out for similar operations in coming years. ✎

Del Rio Vineyards & Winery

Most vintners regard growing and harvesting grapes as backbreaking work, a labor of love. To Rob and Jolee Wallace, managing a vineyard in Oregon was a far less grueling alternative to farming a few thousand acres of tomatoes and rice in California. The climate in Sacramento, Rob points out, enables year-round farming. At least the four-season cycle in southern Oregon allows for periods of rest.

Not that the Wallaces have been kicking back since they moved north to Gold Hill in 2000. They came to manage Del Rio Vineyards at the invitation of family friend and co-owner Lee Traynham, but their achievements extend well beyond land stewardship. In the years following their move, the Wallaces expanded and refined the plantings Traynham had sown after ripping out the old pear orchards, built relationships with dozens of respected wineries around Oregon, transformed an old hotel into a charming tasting room, and established a winery of their own.

The Wallaces were not big wine enthusiasts prior to their career change, but they knew farming. Rob Wallace is a fourth-generation farmer, and he relishes every aspect of coaxing intensely flavored vinifera grapes from the rugged Rogue Valley. Jolee, a former schoolteacher, effortlessly slipped into her role as the face of Del Rio, spearheading improvement projects, ingratiating the winery with the community, and managing the tasting room. Their combination of grit, savvy, and premium grapes earned Del Rio a sterling reputation among winemakers, and it is also gaining recognition as a tourist destination.

The property boasts an unusually rich heritage. In the late 1850s, John White received the land as compensation for his service in the Rogue Indian Wars. He sold the site to another man named White a few years later. Lytte J. White saw an opportunity to establish Rock Point (now Gold Hill) as a tourist draw, a vision made possible by the nearby rail depot. He erected the Rock Point Hotel and Stage Stop in 1864 and did just fine until the railroad altered its route in 1871. In 1907, new owners bought the hotel and surrounding land, planting eight hundred acres with fruit and nuts. Del Rio Orchards rode the Rogue Valley pear boom, flourishing until the Great Depression took hold.

The orchards remained productive for decades but never yielded the kind of profits seen in the early twentieth century. The former hotel was fairly dilapidated by the time the Wallaces arrived, but it was only a matter of months before, with typical industriousness, they set about renovating it into a tasting room. Del Rio didn't start producing its own wine until 2004, instead offering wines made by the wineries to which it sold its grapes. Today the refurbished clapboard building exclusively pours the Del Rio label—served with delicious cheeses from nearby Rogue Creamery.

Aglow with honey-hued woodwork, the tasting room features original flooring and doors; the bar was constructed with timber from the second story, which was not remodeled. Though only one door is in use, you'll notice three doors on the street side of the one-time hotel. Jolee explains that the central door once served as the main entrance, and the ones flanking it led to separate men's and women's parlors, a standard convention in Victorian times.

Other vestiges of the past include historical black-and-white photographs lining the tasting room and the original Del Rio fruit-packing barn, which now houses winery operations. Adjacent to the vineyards is a cemetery where both White families were laid to rest. Energetic visitors will enjoy wandering through the vineyards on routes that lead to the cemetery and a pavilion the Wallaces created in a grove of madrone trees, a restful place for a picnic when no other events are occupying the space. The pretty garden alongside the tasting room is another ideal picnicking spot.

Del Rio's success in raising and selling high-quality fruit—14 varietals on 135 acres—bolsters not only its bottom line, but also the reputation of southern Oregon wineries. By supplying grapes to first-rate wineries such as Domaine Serene, Ken Wright Cellars, and Penner-Ash, Del Rio forces wine watchers to pay attention to this overlooked corner and to contemplate what else the region may be capable of producing.

The area still flies somewhat under the radar of wine enthusiasts, though the Wallaces report that more

---

DEL RIO VINEYARDS & WINERY // 52 N. River Road, P.O. Box 906, Gold Hill, OR 97525

T 541.855.2062
F 541.855.1222
E rob@delriovineyards.com

www.delriovineyards.com

ACCESS
About 16 miles north of Medford. From Interstate 5 south- or northbound, take exit 43. Turn east onto Highway 99, crossing the Rogue River. Turn left on N. River Road and take the first right into Del Rio.

Hours open for visits and tasting: 11AM–5PM daily September–May; 11AM–6PM daily June–August. Closed on major holidays.

TASTINGS & TOURS
$5 for all current releases.

Tours: Appointment necessary for tour. Drop-in tours also available Saturdays in summer.

Typical wines offered: Claret, Cabernet Sauvignon, Merlot, Cabernet Franc, Viognier, Pinot Gris, Rosé Jolee, Syrah, and Chardonnay.

Sales of wine-related items.

PICNICS & PROGRAMS
Picnic area open to the public. Picnic tables on lawn just outside the tasting room and at the upper madrone grove pavilion. No picnic ingredients sold in tasting room.

Special events: Thanksgiving and Mother's Day weekend wine tastings; continuous art shows.

Wine club.

Californians are fleeing the crowded touring scene in Napa to check out the relaxed tasting rooms in the Rogue and Applegate valleys. Locals have also embraced the growing legion of wineries in their midst, happy to see land planted with grapes rather than parceled into subdivisions, and proud to show off their wineries to out-of-town guests. However, southern Oregon won't remain a secret for long: the time to visit is now. ❧

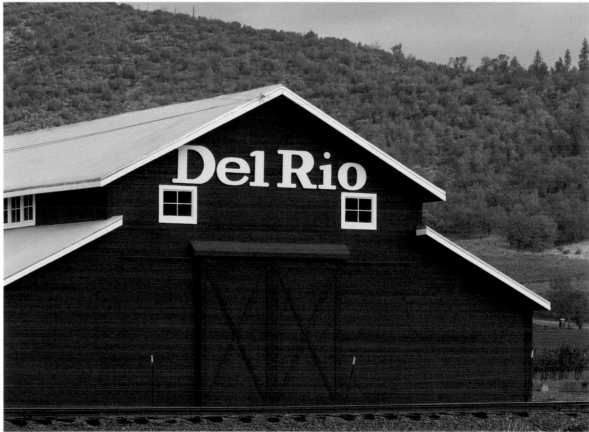

Domaine Drouhin Oregon

OWNERS: THE DROUHIN FAMILY // WINEMAKER: VÉRONIQUE DROUHIN–BOSS

Outspoken winemaker Dick Erath, a founding father of the Willamette Valley wine scene, once quipped that he was relieved to find Domaine Drouhin's first vintage tasted like Oregon Pinot Noir—not French Burgundy. He needn't have worried. The Drouhin family is well versed in the importance of *terroir*, the evanescent forces of dirt, geography, and climate that make an Oregon truffle taste different than one dug up in Provence, or make a Yamhill County Pinot Noir distinct from wine made from the same kind of grapes grown on Burgundy's gravelly slopes.

The Drouhin name is familiar to wine buffs. Joseph Drouhin founded his eponymous wine-shipping company in 1880. Over the next century, second- and third-generation Drouhins Maurice and Robert acquired vineyards, expanded the business, and solidified Drouhin's reputation as a great house of Burgundy.

Robert Drouhin developed an interest in Oregon's nascent wine scene during visits to the West Coast in the 1960s and '70s. He was impressed by the early efforts of Eyrie Vineyards and Adelsheim Vineyard and saw the potential to make superb Pinot Noir in Oregon. Drouhin grew keener on Willamette Valley Pinot Noir when one of Eyrie's wines was the surprise winner—beating out premier Burgundies—at a now-legendary blind tasting held in Paris in 1979. The following year, Drouhin staged a blind tasting at his cellars in Beaune, pitting top Oregon Pinots against Drouhin Grand Crus. This time an Eyrie wine came in second, placing Oregon in the spotlight of a stunned and curious international wine press.

West Coast winemakers often go abroad to work harvest at renowned châteaux in France, but the tables turned in 1986 when Robert Drouhin's daughter Véronique came to Oregon and interned at Adelsheim, Eyrie, and Bethel Heights. She had just earned an advanced degree in enology at the University of Dijon and wanted to gain experience in a region that was still in an experimental phase. She didn't guess that it was only the first of many Oregon vintages she would have a hand in producing.

Véronique returned to the Willamette Valley with her father the following year to evaluate a piece of land that David Adelsheim had suggested they might be interested in buying. The Drouhins did their due diligence on the hundred-acre Dundee Hills property, formerly planted with wheat and Christmas trees, and decided to go for it. Their embrace of the Willamette Valley served notice to the wine world to pay attention to the scrappy Left Coast region. Now that such an esteemed producer of Burgundy had placed his faith in Oregon soil, skeptics were forced to consider—or reconsider—Northwest wines.

For its part, Domaine Drouhin hasn't weathered much skepticism. Winemaker Véronique Drouhin-Boss crafted the estate's first vintage in 1988, using purchased grapes and rented production space, while waiting for her land to be cleared and the winery to be built.

Completed in 1989, it was the first gravity-flow-style winery in Oregon, and it must be the most spotless production facility anywhere. Three types of stainless steel fermenting tanks, several of them empty depending on the time of year, gleam in the lofty, well-lit facility. Véronique favors small open-top tanks for the rich texture they impart, large open-top fermenters that encourage complex aromas to develop, and large sealed tanks for enhanced color extraction. Domaine Drouhin requires extra tanks because it keeps the fruit from individual vineyard blocks separate from harvest through fermentation and barrel aging.

In the barrel cellar beneath the production room, guests will see further evidence of Drouhin's obsession with details. Barrels bear the insignia of François Frères, the cooperage the Drouhin family has worked with since 1900. The company forms custom Petit Drouhin barrels, constructed of oak staves aged for two to four years and cut from trees the Drouhins personally select. Following Burgundian tradition, the winery ages its Chardonnay and Pinot Noir for two and a half to three years between harvest and release, longer than many New World producers. In addition to aging in barrels, the wine rests for months after it has been bottled to let the wine adjust to its new environment.

Domaine Drouhin makes only Pinot Noir and Chardonnay, subscribing to the family mantra to keep things simple and produce the best wines possible—a formula that, for over 125 years, has served the vintners well. With the focus on winemaking, not entertaining, Domaine Drouhin didn't post regular visiting hours until May 2004. The response has been great, and the reasons are plain. For one thing, it is a beautiful hilltop estate. Second, visiting Drouhin is a chance to try truly wonderful wines. But the tours seal the deal. The ninety-minute experience includes an enlightening overview of the winery's philosophy, practices, and history, as well as a comparative tasting of Joseph Drouhin and Domaine Drouhin Oregon wines, accompanied by an assortment of yummy cheeses. It does not disappoint. ↩

60

DOMAINE DROUHIN OREGON // 6750 Breyman Orchards Road, Dayton, OR 97114

T 503.864.2700
F 503.864.3377
E info@domainedrouhin.com

www.domainedrouhin.com

ACCESS
About 45–60 minutes from Portland. From Portland, take Interstate 5 south to exit 294. Turn right onto Highway 99W and follow it through Newberg and Dundee. About 3 miles past Dundee, look for a weigh station on the right. Turn right on McDougall Road and take the first right onto Breyman Orchards Road. Follow it nearly 2 miles to the winery entrance.

Hours open for visits and tasting:
11AM–4PM Wednesday–Sunday, except major holidays.

TASTINGS & TOURS
$5, refunded with purchase of $120 or more.

Tours: $20 for a 90-minute tour, including comparative tasting of Drouhin wines from Oregon and Burgundy with assorted cheeses. Appointment necessary.

Typical wines offered: Pinot Noir and Chardonnay.

No sales of wine-related items.

PICNICS & PROGRAMS
No picnic area open to the public.

Special events: For the Love of Wine Valentine's Day Celebration; Dundee Hills Passport Tour in April; Memorial Weekend Open House; Thanksgiving in Wine Country.

Wine club.

Erath Vineyards

OWNER: **STE. MICHELLE WINE ESTATES** // WINEMAKER: GARY HORNER

Start a conversation about Oregon Pinot Noir and it's not long before the name Erath comes up. Charismatic and straight-talking, Dick Erath won many fans not only for his earthy Pinot Noirs, but also for his unpretentious, dirt-under-the-fingernails approach to winemaking. A member of the first wave of Willamette Valley winemakers, he left California in 1967 for a more fickle proving ground to the north.

Erath caught the wine bug while exploring Napa Valley in the early 1960s. It was during these countryside forays that he first made the connection between great wine and delicious food, a marriage that would guide his winemaking style and company vision. Erath grew up in Oakland and came of age in the beatnik heyday, dabbling in jazz and photography before pursuing a career in the buttoned-down field of electronics. He planted his first vines and crushed his first grapes on a few acres in the semirural Bay Area enclave of Walnut Creek. Erath gradually hooked up with other budding winemakers and enrolled in a two-week enology class at UC Davis. Here he met or heard of Oregon pioneers Richard Sommer, Charles Coury, and David Lett. The frontiersman in him grew excited by the prospect of growing grapes in uncharted territory.

In 1968, Erath acquired two tracts of land, one in the Eola Hills and a larger plot in the Dundee Hills, where he later built a home and winery. The following spring he planted a few acres of Pinot Noir, Riesling, and Gewürztraminer on land he and friends had cleared of old walnut trees. In that first year, Erath's vines were infested by twig borers, soaked by uncharacteristic August rains, and collapsed by a rare Thanksgiving freeze. Tough breaks, but for Erath and a handful of other determined farmers, it was only the beginning of a trying era of figuring out how to grow wine grapes in Oregon.

Still, Erath reaped his initial harvest in 1972 and built a winery next to his home in 1976. Today, Dick and Joan Erath live atop the Prince Hill vineyard, and their old cedar kit house serves as office space. The winery has grown considerably since the '70s: the original structure was expanded to encompass the current tasting room, and a series of barns cropped up over the years to contain Erath's ever-growing production. Though the Dundee Hills setting is impressive, with a pretty vine-covered patio and views of Mounts Jefferson and Hood, the estate is not a dazzler. Instead, it bears all the signs of a working winery, with fermentation tanks crammed into simple, boxy sheds and hoses running in every direction. The wood-paneled tasting room and a stand of massive fir trees complete a rustic über-Oregon tableau. Very Dick Erath.

Erath loves to cook and considers wine an essential component of a satisfying meal. In 2005, he helped initiate a series of chef-winemakers' dinners at the sumptuous new Black Walnut Inn, just down the road from the winery. Part of the mission is to demonstrate the wines' compatibility with flavors that roam from serrano chile to maitake mushroom. Pinot Noir composes the bulk of Erath's wine portfolio, but the winery also produces a fair amount of Pinot Gris and, in lesser quantities, Pinot Blanc—all are valued for their food-pairing versatility. (Erath also makes small amounts of Dolcetto, Riesling, and Gewürztraminer, available only at the tasting room.) Because Dick Erath believes you can't really have a decent meal without wine, the winery offers two tiers of product: affordable varietals it deems Monday-through-Friday sippers and more expressive (and expensive) reserve and single-vineyard wines for indulgent weekend dinners.

Pinot Noir is an expensive wine to craft, but one of Dick Erath's enduring goals is to make a high-quality, under-twenty-dollar bottle. Erath's flagship Oregon Pinot Noir series is the result, and it now accounts for three-quarters of the winery's annual seventy-thousand-case output. To manage costs, the wine is fermented in stainless-steel containers fitted with oak staves instead of in oak barrels, which run about eight hundred to a thousand dollars apiece. (Estate and single-vineyard Pinots are barrel-aged, however.)

Erath makes wine with fruit from its 115 estate acres, sourcing additional grapes from various Oregon growers. The winery's production doubled between 2002 and 2006; in 2005 alone, sales of Pinot Noir grew by nearly 100 percent. Oregon wineries credit the movie *Sideways* (in which the protagonist derides Merlot and eloquently makes a case for Pinot Noir) for generating instant, unprecedented demand for the wine. But Pinot Noir producers also say interest was mounting in 2004 as consumers recognized the wine's genius for complementing food. For its part, Erath will ride the wave as long as it can. ∾

(Ed. note: Ste. Michelle Wine Estates purchased Erath Vineyards in May 2006. Dick Erath will continue to oversee the vineyard.)

ERATH VINEYARDS // 9409 N.E. Worden Hill Road, Dundee, OR 97115

T 800.539.9463; 503.538.3318
F 503.538.1074
E info@erath.com

www.erath.com

ACCESS
About 45 minutes from Portland. From Portland, take Interstate 5 south to exit 294. Turn right onto Highway 99W and follow it through Newberg to Dundee. In Dundee, turn right onto Ninth Street, which becomes Worden Hill Road. Continue 2.5 miles to the winery.

Hours open for visits and tasting: 11AM–5PM daily, except Easter, Thanksgiving Day, Christmas Day, and New Year's Day.

TASTINGS & TOURS
Complimentary tasting of Oregon series of wines; $5 to taste estate and single-vineyard Pinot Noirs.

Tours: Appointment necessary.

Typical wines offered: Pinot Noir, Pinot Gris, and Pinot Blanc.

Sales of wine-related items.

PICNICS & PROGRAMS
Picnic area open to the public on the patio. Picnic ingredients sold in tasting room, including smoked salmon, assorted cheeses, and crackers.

Special events: Dundee Hills Passport Tour in April; Memorial Weekend Open House; Thanksgiving in Wine Country; Erath Chef Series of seasonal dinners at the nearby Black Walnut Inn.

Wine club.

King Estate Winery

OWNERS: **THE KING FAMILY** // WINEMAKER: **BILL KREMER**

On misty days when rain makes Oregon forests appear almost prehistorically lush, driving west on Camas Swale Road creates the impression of traveling deep into a land of gnomes and nymphs. Small, close-in hills dictate a road full of S-curves that shuttles you past low-lying sheep pastures, tumbledown cottages, and moss-covered trees. Turning onto Territorial Road, you're shocked out of this woodsy trance by a landscape of wide-open fields. Then comes the biggest surprise of all: a grand hilltop estate dramatically framed by hundreds of acres of vines.

With the completion in October 2005 of a visitor center as large as some airports, King Estate is one of the most impressive stops on a tour of Beaver State wineries. The sprawling ochre stucco buildings combine traditional château architecture with the timber detailing common in the Northwest, for a contemporary effect.

Until late 2005, King Estate had a tasting room the size of a walk-in closet, which hardly suited the grandeur and aspirations of the winery—one of Oregon's five largest. Now a concierge greets visitors at the entrance of the ornate tasting facility, assisting with case sales and questions. Straight ahead stands the semicircular hemlock-trimmed bar, where cheerful young servers pour wine in a setting surely a hundred times more lavish than their collegiate crash pads. A cozy hearth room, lit by alabaster sconces and furnished with leather couches and a library of wine books, invites lounging. Rustic fir post-and-beam construction complements stained concrete flooring and a sturdy radiant-heat soapstone fireplace that includes a hatch for baking bread.

A pair of King Estate cookbooks—*New American Cuisine Pinot Gris Cookbook* and *King Estate Pinot Noir Cookbook*—attests that the commercial kitchen concealed behind the bar does more than bake bread. The culinary program emphasizes organic produce grown within the 541 area code, executing meals for bistro customers, the production crew, and corporate groups that convene in the well-equipped retreat rooms upstairs.

For a bit of historical perspective, check out the black-and-white photographs hung throughout the center; some depict the 1910 Lorane baseball team, while others show hops pickers, evidence of an earlier beverage industry that once dominated this stretch of countryside. The land later supported orchards and various vegetables, crops that are still profitable today. To showcase the rich growing region, King Estate opened a handsome red barn marketplace, also in the fall of 2005, vending its own potatoes, pumpkins, fruit, and honey, plus goods from local purveyors. Located about halfway up King Estate's long driveway, the marketplace also hosts wine tastings and guest speakers, albeit in a more casual setting than the visitor center.

A love for the land—and shrewd business sense—forms the basis of King Estate. Ed King III, a Kansas City businessman who relocated to the Eugene area in the late '80s, was driving the Lane County back roads, looking for hay for his horses, when he noticed the south-facing slopes that now yield King Estate grapes. After studying the soils, which turned out to be well-drained Jory and Bellpine composition, King and his father, Ed King Jr., began drafting a long-range plan to plant vineyards and build a winery.

The winery was completed in 1992, the year of its first vintage, and the property has expanded to include 1,033 acres, 250 of which are planted with vines. In addition to cultivating Pinot Gris, Chardonnay, and Pinot Noir vines (Pinot Gris accounts for 60 percent of winery production), King Estate established Lorane Grapevines, a vine-propagation operation for rearing various phylloxera-resistant rootstocks to use at King Estate and sell to other vineyards around the country. (Phylloxera are tiny aphidlike insects that attack the roots of grapevines and interrupt the flow of nutrients and water, and they are a serious threat to commercial vineyards worldwide.) This plant diversity gives winemaker Bill Kremer plenty of raw materials to play with, allowing him to produce experimental blends and varietals, which are available to taste or purchase only at the visitor center. Craftsman-series wines, including Cabernet Sauvignon, Merlot, Gewürztraminer, and hefty one-and-a-half-, three-, and five-liter bottles of King's popular varietals, are also sold at the winery.

Wines are further classified as Signature and Domaine bottlings. Signature wines are made with estate grapes and fruit purchased from vineyards in the Willamette and Rogue valleys, while limited-edition Domaine selections are handcrafted with the best grapes plucked from King's onsite certified organic vineyards.

Visitors can witness some of the work that goes into these bottlings during a guided tour of the winery. The massive 110,000-square-foot facility is designed to handle a maximum of 125,000 cases, which King Estate—whose wines are distributed in all fifty states and Mexico—will reach before long. Tours travel past the crush pad and into a large barn holding fermentation and blending tanks, and then transition to the striking barrel cellar. It's an enchanting chamber with creamy walls and a softly arched ceiling. Last stop is the patio, perfectly positioned to let you feast on views of the vineyards, an old pioneer cemetery, and the valley beyond—as well as on a few small plates from the bistro.

KING ESTATE WINERY // 80854 Territorial Road, Eugene, OR 97405

T 800.884.4441; 541.942.9874
F 541.942.9867
E info@kingestate.com

www.kingestate.com

ACCESS
About 20 miles southwest of Eugene. From Interstate 5 southbound, take exit 182 at Creswell. Head west on Oregon Avenue, which becomes Camas Swale Road and then Ham Road. Turn left at Territorial Highway and travel 2.5 miles to the winery. From Interstate 5 northbound, take exit 162. Turn right onto Curtin Road and then left on Territorial Highway. Follow it 10 miles to the winery.

Hours open for visits and tasting:
Noon–5PM daily, except major holidays.

TASTINGS & TOURS
No charge for tasting.

Tours: Guided tours at 1, 2, 3, and 4PM Friday–Sunday. Drop-in tours Monday–Thursday, staff permitting. No appointment necessary.

Typical wines offered: Pinot Gris, Pinot Noir, and Chardonnay. Limited releases include Vin Gris (rosé) and Vin Glacé (ice wine).

Sales of wine-related items.

PICNICS & PROGRAMS
Picnic area open to the public on the patio and by the oak grove. Picnic ingredients sold in tasting room.

Special events: Frequent culinary workshops; annual open houses and barrel tastings Memorial Day and Thanksgiving weekends.

Wine club.

Sokol Blosser Winery

Susan Sokol and Bill Blosser met at Stanford in the late 1960s while pursuing liberal arts degrees. They married and moved to Dundee because Bill had secured a teaching job at Portland State University. Though they had no experience working in a vineyard, they decided to try their hands at growing grapes—in a region that had yet to be colonized by winegrowers. And they decided to focus on Pinot Noir, a grape that had not really been cultivated in the United States. But they were young and emboldened by the notion that anything was possible.

"When I look back on starting out—my husband, Bill, and I were in our twenties—I can see that maybe we were part of the back-to-the-land movement that was taking place at the time," Susan says. "We weren't full-blown hippies, but we wanted to produce something from the land."

The Blossers discovered they were part of another movement afoot in the Dundee Hills in the early 1970s, set in motion by a group of pioneers who would shape the state's wine industry. Like-minded couples including the Letts (Eyrie Vineyards), Adelsheims, Eraths, and Ponzis all settled in Yamhill County around the same time with the intention of growing Pinot Noir. "We shared ideas and stuck together; there was a real closeness among us," Susan remembers. "There was a time when [everyone in the] Oregon wine industry fit in any one of our living rooms."

It sounds romantic, and it probably was to some extent, but as any entrepreneur knows, carving something out of nothing is hard work. "During the decade of the '70s, we planted a vineyard, started a winery, and had three kids," Susan says. She recounts her remarkable story in a new memoir, *At Home in the Vineyard: Cultivating a Winery, an Industry, and a Life* (University of California Press, 2006).

The CliffsNotes version goes something like this: The Blossers first planted grapes in 1971, supplying fruit to winemakers like Dick Erath and David Lett. They liked their friends' wines and soon realized that making wine was their logical next step. Susan's father, a wine lover who helped his daughter cultivate an appreciation for Bordeaux and Burgundy, came on as a partner, providing crucial financial support. Sokol Blosser produced its first vintage in 1977, and the tasting room opened to visitors the following year.

Designed by architect John Storrs, who also drafted the landmark Oregon resort Salishan, it was the first purpose-built tasting room in the state. It is not a stately monument that commands your attention. Rather, the wooden structure harmonizes with the landscape, underscoring the company's strong environmental ethos. More rustic than some, it *feels* like Oregon. Nestled among old oak trees, it extends to a large deck for picnicking and is surrounded by a colorful mix of lavender, poppies, and yarrow.

Today Sokol Blosser is one of the most visited wineries in the region; to accommodate the twenty-five thousand tourists who visit each year, plans are under way to expand the facility. At the time it was built, tasting rooms were rare and generally makeshift, but Susan foresaw the importance of teaching visitors about what goes into making wine and the economic advantage of direct-to-consumer sales. Though the winery doesn't offer regular tours, it hands out instructive literature to guide visitors through a unique test vineyard. Situated next to the parking lot, the small plot of vines was planted in 1974 to test various clones obtained from the Colmar Viticultural Station in Alsace. A pamphlet describes the grapes, which include Pinot Noir as well as less familiar varieties such as Müller-Thurgau, named for the Swiss professor who developed it in the 1880s. The guide also discusses typical vineyard activity season by season.

Sokol Blosser has long embraced sustainable farming and business practices, and its estate vineyards received USDA organic certification from Oregon Tilth in 2005. In 2002, it became the first American winery to earn LEED (Leadership in Energy and Environmental Design) certification for its very cool barrel cellar, which is naturally insulated by soil and has a living roof covered with wildflowers. "We've always tried to be sensitive to the environment, but we've become more stringent in how we define that," Susan says. "Every decision we make, whether it's remodeling or buying toilet paper, is done with sustainability in mind."

SOKOL BLOSSER WINERY // 5000 Sokol Blosser Lane, P.O. Box 399, Dundee, OR 97115

T 800.582.6668; 503.864.2282
F 503.864.2710
E info@sokolblosser.com

www.sokolblosser.com

ACCESS
About 45 minutes from Portland. From Portland, take Interstate 5 south to exit 294 at Tigard. Turn right onto Highway 99W and continue on 99W through Tigard, Newberg, and Dundee. Turn right at the blue sign about 2 miles outside Dundee. Follow the lane a short distance to the winery.

Hours open for visits and tasting: 11AM–5PM daily, except major holidays.

TASTINGS & TOURS
$5 to $15, depending on choice of wines.

Tours: No regular tours.

Typical wines offered: Pinot Noir, Pinot Gris, Rosé of Pinot Noir, Evolution (proprietary white blend of nine grapes), and Meditrina (proprietary red blend of Pinot Noir, Syrah, and Zinfandel).

Sales of wine-related items.

PICNICS & PROGRAMS
Picnic area open to the public on the deck. Picnic ingredients sold in tasting room, including smoked salmon, cheeses, crackers, and Dagoba chocolate.

Special events: Dundee Hills Passport Tour in April; Memorial Weekend Wine Tasting Party; Thanksgiving in Wine Country; themed seasonal events, such as Meditrina Day in October, throughout the year.

Wine club.

Other goals, like the ambition to make seductive Pinot Noir, remain constant. The majority of Sokol Blosser's eighty acres are given over to Pinot Noir, and the winery has always focused on the varietal, but it struggles to keep its Pinot identity front and center due to the striking success of its other wines.

Like many runaway hits, Evolution, its most popular wine, was a bit of a fluke. One of the clones Sokol Blosser experimented with was Müller-Thurgau, which doesn't exactly roll off the tongue. A friend's suggestion to give the wine a proprietary name led to the creation of a food-friendly white blend that combines nine grapes and was first released in 1998. Then, after customers requested a red version of Evolution, Sokol Blosser created Meditrina, a silky combination of Pinot Noir, Syrah, and Zinfandel, which came out in 2004.

These everyday wines are fun and affordable. They're not as serious as Sokol Blosser's single-block Pinot Noirs, but if they bring more wine drinkers into the fold, that's a good thing. ৯

Valley View Winery

OWNERS: MARK & MICHAEL WISNOVSKY // WINEMAKER: JOHN GUERRERO

If you don't know Syrah from Sangiovese and have never even heard of Viognier, don't worry. Valley View Winery welcomes you with open arms. Though this southern Oregon winery crafts premium wine, it emphasizes value and transparency, targeting the casual sipper who is more interested in drinking than in deconstructing wine.

It's a refreshingly grounded approach, reflecting the straight-shooting candor of owners Mark and Mike Wisnovsky, who now run the winery their father started in the early 1970s. The Wisnovskys are in this business to make a living, a factor that defines most small, family-run wineries and distinguishes them in terms of presentation and attitude from larger operations—which sometimes lack a personal quality. At Valley View, you'll often find the brothers pouring wine behind the copper-topped circular bar or taking orders over the phone.

Jacksonville town founder Peter Britt first planted grapes in the Applegate Valley in the 1850s, and the fancy fruit outfit Harry and David began harvesting its coveted Comice pears in 1910, blazing the trail for future viticulturists. Southern Oregon enjoys extended summer sunlight and cool nights, conditions that permit grapes to ripen slowly and hang on the vine longer. Slow ripening coaxes along concentrated flavor without incurring sky-high sugar levels, which can contribute an undesirable, hotly alcoholic quality to wine. The region also offers plentiful valley sites with south-facing slopes, altitudes ranging from one thousand to fifteen hundred feet, and consistent airflow that wards off mold and encourages steady ripening. In other words, the climate and topography are ideal for growing Bordeaux varietals.

These attributes prompted Frank Wisnovsky to relocate his family from New Jersey to Jacksonville in 1971. He studied weather records available from the historical society and convinced an alfalfa farmer to sell his seventy-seven-acre plot, complete with a charming turn-of-the-century pole barn. Wisnovsky, a civil engineer, had become interested in wine while temporarily living in the Bay Area to design a suspension system for the underwater Bay Area Rapid Transit tunnels. He enrolled in an extension class in enology at UC Davis, and learned that the Applegate Valley had supported vineyards a century earlier.

Like many vintners who are getting to know their land, Wisnovsky planted his first twelve acres with a range of vines, including Merlot, Pinot Noir, and Gamay Noir. Valley View made its first wine in 1976, crafting it at Tualatin Estates Winery; its premier on-site bottling came two years later. While Valley View experimented with varietals, it also started reaping praise. "Cabernet Sauvignon really carried us in the beginning," Mike Wisnovsky says. "We developed a local following right away when the Jacksonville Inn started serving it. The Inn was our first customer, and it's still a great customer."

Valley View still sells primarily to locals, doing brisk trade in its airy Craftsman-style tasting room. In fact, half of the winery's ten-thousand-case annual production is sold directly to consumers. Online sales are not particularly robust. "We have a slightly older consumer who may not use the Internet that much," Mike says. "On a whim, I started calling up regular customers to see if they needed to restock, and people loved that personal touch."

Recognizing the influx of wineries and tourists to the area, Valley View knew it needed a grand tasting room to accommodate visitor traffic, and completed its onsite wine pavilion in the fall of 2001. The expansive peaked-roof building comprises offices, the tasting bar, a banquet room, retail, and a patio for warm-weather loafing. The winery also has maintained a tasting-room presence, in one form or another, for over twenty years in downtown Jacksonville; currently the fancy foods store Jacksonville Mercantile exclusively pours Valley View wines.

After Frank Wisnovsky died in a diving accident in 1980, his wife, Ann Wisnovsky, kept the winery going until Mark started to run the family business in 1988. A couple of years later, Valley View sent its barrel-select Chardonnay to the World Wine Championship in Slovenia. It unexpectedly won a double gold, and Valley View received major media attention for the first time. This achievement prompted the creation of the Anna Maria label—in honor of the family matriarch—denoting Valley View's finest wines. Valley View bestows the Anna Maria label only when a wine exceeds its expectations; some years, just a few varietals attain Anna Maria status. Other years, none do.

Anna Maria wines cost more than the Valley View series, but they are still quite reasonable, falling mostly in the twenty- to thirty-dollar range. The winery makes the distinction plain to customers, promoting its Valley View label as weekday wines and Anna Maria selections as special-occasion drinkers. "Our customers don't read *Wine Spectator* and may know very little about wine, but they know what they like," Mike says. "They enjoy cooking and like to have wine every day without breaking the bank—and they're confident in their palates." ❧

VALLEY VIEW WINERY // 1000 Upper Applegate Road, Jacksonville, OR 97530

T 800.781.9463; 541.899.8468
F 541.899.8468
E valleyviewwinery@charter.net

www.valleyviewwinery.com

ACCESS
About 9 miles from Jacksonville town center. From Jacksonville, head south on Route 238 for nearly 7 miles. Turn left on Upper Applegate Road and follow it 1 mile to the winery on the right.

Hours open for visits and tasting: 11AM–5PM daily, except major holidays.

TASTINGS & TOURS
No charge for tasting.

No tours.

Typical wines offered: Merlot, Cabernet Sauvignon, Chardonnay, Syrah, Viognier, and Pinot Gris.

Sales of wine-related items.

PICNICS & PROGRAMS
Picnic area open to the public on the patio and overlooking the vineyards. Picnic ingredients sold in tasting room. Numerous locally produced cheeses, crackers, buffalo sausage, juice, bottled water, and other drinks are available.

Special events: Spring and fall case sales; periodic art and live-music shows.

Wine club.

When Willamette Valley Vineyards founder Jim Bernau started scouting land on which to plant Pinot Noir and Pinot Gris in the early 1980s, conventional wisdom pointed to the volcanic soils in Dundee, where pioneering winemakers were successfully coaxing along the finicky varietals. But Bernau wanted south-facing slopes at a slightly higher elevation, the altitude of Grand Cru vineyards in Burgundy's Côte d'Or. He was considering a tract of land blanketed by scotch broom and blackberry brambles just south of Salem when he had a fortuitous encounter with a neighbor. The woman's great-grandfather had farmed plums on the land, she told Bernau, but her family had had a hard time making a living because the earth would yield only small whiskey prunes.

"Well, my heart was pounding," Bernau recalls, when he learned that the hillside had a history of producing tight, concentrated fruit—not so desirable to plum farmers, perhaps, but pure gold to grape growers. Bernau's faith in the land's potential turned out to be more than a hunch, and after purchasing that initial plot, he bought up adjacent patches to amass fifty acres of vineyards. Equally important to Willamette Valley Vineyards' success, Bernau had the good sense to snap up Tualatin Estates' eighty acres when grower Bill Fuller retired in 1997. Located near Forest Grove, Tualatin Estates boasts some of the oldest Pinot Noir vines in Oregon. Bernau increased planting at this property, doubling its vineyard acreage and propelling Willamette Valley Vineyards toward an annual production of about ninety thousand cases.

A leading producer of both Pinot Noir and Pinot Gris, Willamette Valley enjoys nationwide distribution and is one of Oregon's most visible labels. (Even episodes of *Friends*, Rachael Ray's *$40 a Day*, and White House dinners have featured the wines.) The winery, just off Interstate 5 near the kitschy theme park Enchanted Forest, isn't hard to spot, either, though its proximity to the freeway doesn't cheapen its striking setting high atop Ilahee Hill.

Accessibility sums up more than just Willamette Valley's location: it is a publicly owned operation, unusual for its size, with group photographs of shareholders proudly displayed in the winery. And affordability is as much a guiding principle as quality. "I want to be the under-fifty-dollar Pinot Noir of choice for America," Bernau says. In fact, Willamette Valley makes several respected Pinots in the neighborhood of twenty dollars.

A visit to the winery makes clear its proletarian leanings. Though it cuts an impressive silhouette—aided by an octagonal lookout tower—amid all that vineyard land, the estate is well worn and informal. The winery was designed for visitors to conduct their own tours, wandering up to the lookout tower, across balconies overlooking the production facility and crush zone, and onto the deck for a picnic. Willamette Valley offers tours by appointment and will accommodate unscheduled tours, which can include impromptu barrel tastings and perhaps even a nip of winemaker Forrest Klaffke's experimental port, if staffing permits. For its size and rank as one of Oregon's most visited wineries, the winery delivers a surprisingly homey, personal experience.

Tours elucidate the winemaking process at Willamette Valley for guests, describing the differences among the soils that characterize its vineyards, detailing grape varieties, and explaining fermentation. But you might also pick up on a few of the winery's quirkier practices, such as its commitment to biodiesel, which fuels its tractors and delivery vans and even employees' personal vehicles.

Bernau, in addition to being an incredibly passionate supporter of Oregon's wine industry as a whole, is a pretty quirky guy himself. He had his first sip of wine as an adolescent in Roseburg when his dad, a lawyer who counted trailblazing vintner Richard Sommer among his clients, brought home a bottle of wine to have with dinner. He remembers his father's sage prediction that someday Oregon would be covered in vines (he probably gleaned this insight from Sommer, who planted the state's first post-Prohibition vineyards in 1957 and founded the Riesling-focused HillCrest Winery). After this eye-opening taste, Bernau and his brother secretly began making wine from grape juice and, eventually, from wine grapes. "There are probably still bottles hidden in the crawlspace of my parents' house. Most of it was terrible!"

Intent on crafting wines that reflect their origin and have the potential to age well, the winery places particular emphasis on soil and vine health. Bernau explains that he relishes the challenging factors—rain, cold, fog—winegrowers face in the Willamette Valley, and he is convinced they contribute to the elegance that defines Oregon-made Burgundian varietals. "California, with all its heat, can make huge, jammy wines. But I'm interested in the difficult elements we have to deal with here." ☙

70

WILLAMETTE VALLEY VINEYARDS // 8800 Enchanted Way S.E., Turner, OR 97392

T 800.344.9463
F 503.588.8894
E info@wvv.com

www.willamettevalleyvineyards.com

ACCESS
About 5 miles south of Salem. From Interstate 5 south- and northbound, take exit 248. Turn onto Delaney Road heading east. Turn right onto Enchanted Way S.E. and continue 1 mile to the winery.

Hours open for visits and tasting:
11AM–6PM daily, except major holidays.

TASTINGS & TOURS
Complimentary vintage tasting; $6 reserve tasting, including a Riedel glass.

Tours: Appointment necessary.

Typical wines offered: Pinot Noir, Pinot Gris, Chardonnay, Riesling, Syrah, and Viognier.

Sales of wine-related items.

PICNICS & PROGRAMS
Picnic area open to the public on the patio and overlooking the vineyards. Picnic ingredients sold in tasting room, including cheese, smoked salmon, nuts, and chocolate.

Special events: Annual Mo's Crab and Chowder Festival in January; Pinot Noir and Chocolate Celebration in February; Annual Wine, Cheese and Pear Jubilee in March; Memorial Weekend Open House; Grape Stomp and Harvest Celebration in late September; Thanksgiving in Wine Country; seasonal dinners and live music.

Wine club.

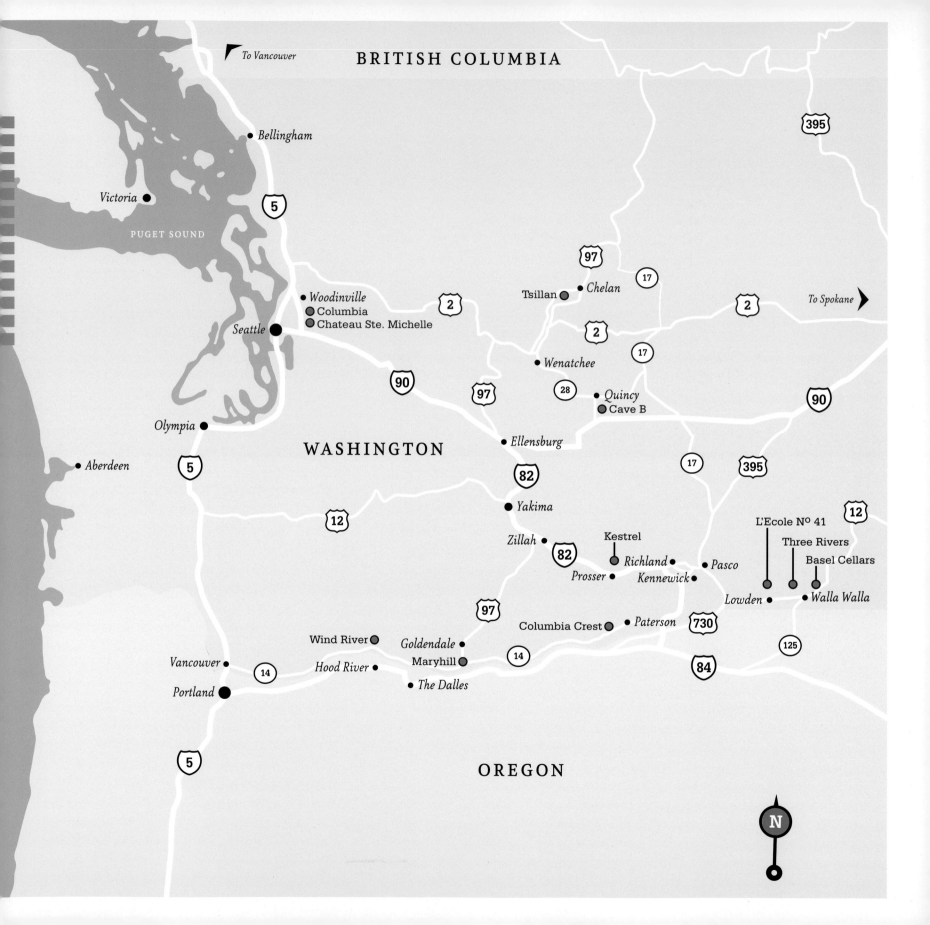

Washington

A popular saying in Washington is that it's the best place on earth to grow grapes. Even outsiders have to agree the adage is not mere puffery. While Washington isn't ideal for every type of wine grape, its climate, geography, and soils conspire to support a throng of varieties, from Sémillon to Syrah. It's no coincidence that the state is second only to California in volume of wine produced in North America. Washington has seen its wineries nearly triple in number since 2000; currently it supports 405 and counting. At one end of the spectrum is Chateau Ste. Michelle—a juggernaut with an annual output far exceeding Oregon's entire case production—but many wineries occupy the opposite end, producing fewer than three thousand cases per year.

One of the most talked-about areas in Washington these days is Walla Walla, a small college town in the southeast. It exemplifies an exciting direction for Washington wine, emphasizing quality over quantity and giving credence to the notion that wine can catapult a community into a new era. It's become a hot destination for wine and food lovers, and the stately limestone buildings on Main Street have reawakened with the glow and bustle of spectacular restaurants. Growth spots such as the Columbia Cascades, the Olympic Peninsula, and the Red Mountain area may soon enjoy similar revivals. ॐ

THE WINERIES

Basel Cellars Estate Winery

Cave B Estate Winery

Chateau Ste. Michelle Vineyards & Winery

Columbia Crest

Columbia Winery

Kestrel Vintners

L'Ecole Nº 41

Maryhill Winery

Three Rivers Winery

Tsillan Cellars

Wind River Cellars

Basel Cellars Estate Winery

OWNERS: GREG & BECKY BASEL AND STEVE & JO MARIE HANSEN // WINEMAKER: TREY BUSCH

Even as showpiece wineries go, Basel Cellars is extravagant. Constructed in the style of grand park lodges, it is a sprawling edifice of natural stone, handcrafted woodwork, and enormous windows. Architectural features include carved mahogany doors, archways composed of hand-waxed twisted juniper trunks, and a small theater with stadium seating. But then, it wasn't designed as a winery; it was built as a private residence during the high-tech boom of the late 1990s. Owners Kyle Mussman, who made his fortune in cellular technology,

and his wife, Lori Mussman, divorced soon after the estate was completed, and the nine-bedroom property went on the market.

Around the same time, Portland contractor Greg Basel retired to Walla Walla on a tract of land adjacent to the renowned Pepper Bridge Vineyard. Basel's neighbor Norm McKibben, the visionary behind Pepper Bridge, encouraged him to take advantage of the rich soil he was sitting on by planting a vineyard as a hobby and investment. Basel raised vines and began selling fruit to wineries. He wasn't planning to go into winemaking but soon realized he could turn a greater profit by producing his own wine than by selling grapes. Business partner Steve Hansen, a fellow alumnus of construction corporation Peter Kiewit Sons' and a passionate oenophile, embraced the idea of a winery, and the partners began casting around for a suitable facility.

It was the garage, not the mansion, that sold Basel on the Mussman residence. Mussman had installed a 9,600-square-foot subterranean structure to house his car collection. After one look, Basel knew it would make an ideal production room. It has a sophisticated temperature control system, automated ventilation to replace harmful carbon dioxide fumes with fresh oxygen, and a level driveway that works perfectly as a crush pad.

Of course, the garage represents only a fraction of the estate footprint—what to do with the home, guest house, outdoor pool, and tennis courts? The residence

includes enough bedrooms to serve as a B&B, but not an equal number of bathrooms. And Basel wanted to focus on the winery, not on running an inn.

The solution? A wine club with unusual benefits. Club members are granted exclusive use of the residence to stage weekend getaways, parties, family reunions, and weddings. Hot summers make the pool-and-cabana setup—complete with hot tub and professional-grade grills—especially attractive. Visit Basel Cellars' tasting room during high season and you're likely to spot revelers lounging in the sun with margaritas—or glasses of Basel's fruity Syrah Rosé.

The winery specializes in Bordeaux varietals, crafting plush, full-bodied Merlot, Cabernet Sauvignon, Cabernet Franc, and Merriment, a blend of all three grapes that is the winery's flagship bottling. Young winemaker Trey Busch, who learned the ropes as assistant winemaker at Walla Walla's respected Dunham Cellars, also makes Syrah, a classic Rhône varietal, and Claret, which is gaining momentum in the Northwest. Also expect to see more Cabernet Franc, traditionally overlooked in favor of jammier Sauvignon; some say this lean, powerful varietal will be Washington's next Syrah.

Busch joined Basel in 2002. The winery opened to the public the following February and was fully operational for the 2003 harvest. It has a fifty-eight-acre estate vineyard and produces about four thousand cases annually, with plans to grow slowly. Basel Cellars' packaging reflects the care that goes into creating its small-production wines. Each bottle is hand-dipped in bronze-colored wax, resulting in an impressive seal more common to fine vessels of bourbon than to wine.

As Basel Cellars adds new wines to its portfolio, the estate changes to accommodate guests and private parties. Until December 2005, the tasting room resided in the original home, an intimate sitting room anchored by a sturdy gnarled-wood bar. It was cordoned off from the rest of the house so as not to interfere with club members' sojourns.

Now the tasting room is inside yet another former garage, adjacent to the house. Designed to hold seven cars, it is a large space with a long bar and several bistro tables; a new wooden floor adds warmth and counteracts the former-garage feeling. Tours of the facility can be arranged in advance, but now visitors miss out on glimpsing the over-the-top interiors of the mansion.

BASEL CELLARS ESTATE WINERY // 2901 Old Milton Highway, Walla Walla, WA 99362

T 509.522.0200
F 509.522.0996
E info@baselcellars.com

www.baselcellars.com

ACCESS
From Interstate 84 eastbound, take exit 179 to Interstate 82W toward Hermiston/Umatilla. Continue to Highway 12 and take exit 113 to Walla Walla. Exit onto Highway 125S toward Pendleton and continue toward Milton-Freewater. Turn right onto Old Milton Highway and go about 1 mile to the winery on the left.

Hours open for visits and tasting: 10AM–4PM Monday–Saturday, 11AM–4PM Sunday, except major holidays.

TASTINGS & TOURS
$5, applicable toward wine purchase.

Tours: Appointment necessary.

Typical wines offered: Claret, Cabernet Sauvignon, Cabernet Franc, Syrah, Merriment (flagship Bordeaux-style blend), Caspia Rosé, and Forget-Me-Not white (fifty-fifty blend of Chardonnay and Sauvignon Blanc).

Sales of wine-related items.

PICNICS & PROGRAMS
Picnic area open to the public. No picnic ingredients sold in tasting room.

Special events: Spring Release Weekend the first weekend of May; Holiday Barrel Tasting the first weekend of December; seasonal winemaker's dinners.

Wine club.

Still, Basel Cellars, situated high on a butte that appears to rise out of nowhere, makes for a memorable visit. You pass through ornate iron gates and make the curvy journey to the top. The Walla Walla River runs to the south of the property, Yellow Hawk Creek to the north. Spotting wild rabbits, coyotes, or yellow hawks is not out of the question. That Busch's velvety, fruit-forward wines make as strong an impression as the lavish estate is testament to Basel Cellars' dedication to quality. ◡

Cave B Estate Winery

OWNERS: **VINCENT & CAROL BRYAN** // WINEMAKER: **BERLE FIGGINS**

The town of George, Washington, is known for two things: a silly name and big-ticket concerts at the Gorge Amphitheater. In time it will also generate buzz as the home of Cave B Estate Winery and the Inn at SageCliffe, an ambitious luxury resort that includes a winery, vineyard, restaurant, spa, golf course, and equestrian center.

The tasteful central Washington encampment is dramatically situated on variegated basalt cliffs nine hundred feet above the Columbia River. Though the winery and resort are just a few years old, owners Vincent and Carol Bryan settled the land in 1980. After traveling around the world, the Bryans felt that few places were as captivating as the Columbia River Gorge. Vince, a neurosurgeon from Mercer Island, dreamed of planting vineyards. After studying the climate, soil composition, and geology of the remote site, he determined that wine grapes would thrive there. The Bryans tried fourteen different varietals, sold the fruit to wineries across the state, and established Champs de Brionne Winery while Vince continued to practice medicine.

They also began the tradition of staging concerts in George. In 1985, the Bryans planned an outdoor celebration to mark the first Champs de Brionne vintage. They invited residents from surrounding rural towns and were stunned to receive hundreds of affirmative replies. Their intended party locale near the vineyards wasn't big enough to accommodate such numbers, so the Bryans moved the event to the couple's favorite picnicking spot, a bowl formation that created a natural amphitheater on their property. The performer was a brass band from Wenatchee.

The party was a hit, and the Bryans realized that concerts were a great means of selling wine. The Gorge at George, boasting fantastic acoustics and mood-enhancing scenery, went on to become one of the country's largest, most sought-after music venues. Winemaking in George, however, flourished in fits and starts.

By 1993, it was time for a break. The Bryans sold the Gorge Amphitheater and some of their acreage, retaining the vineyards. They decamped to Capri, Italy, for some downtime, but characteristically, Dr. Bryan wasn't content to merely relax. It was there that he began sketching a replacement spinal-column disc, an invention that brought the Bryans a fair bit of financial security. They didn't foresee opening another winery, but by 2000, they felt the pull of the grape. They envisioned a center for the culinary sciences and wine education, a retreat for artists, scientists, and foodies. Windfall at the ready, the Bryans began laying plans for a sumptuous resort that would feed their passions and celebrate the agricultural bounty and wines of Washington.

Seattle architect Tom Kundig designed the first wave of the minivillage: an airy main lodge with three suites, fifteen private cottages, and twelve sequestered cavern rooms fitted into hillside nooks. Barrel roofs, giant windows, and rock exteriors help the structures harmonize with the craggy, sage-covered landscape. The lodge and rooms are comfortably modern on the inside, featuring stone fireplaces, decorative glass flourishes, and leather furniture. The winery, with a temperature-regulating earth-covered roof, appears to rise out of the ground.

Consulting winemaker Brian Carter started crafting wines with estate grapes, making just a few barrels. In 2002, the winery and tasting room were completed, Carter upped production, and Cave B, named for the Bryans, was under way. Soon, Berle (Rusty) Figgins joined the operation as winemaker and, with viticulturist Jeff Cleveringa, began grafting over vines with varietals better suited to the property. Walla Walla native Figgins learned the ropes at famed Leonetti Cellar—the winery his brother Gary Figgins founded in 1978—then served as winemaker of Northstar Winery and founded Glen Fiona, one of the first Washington houses to focus on Syrah. Credentials like these should garner much attention for Cave B and the Columbia Cascade winegrowing region in the coming years.

Figgins focuses on the classic Bordeaux varietals Merlot and Cabernet Sauvignon, as well as Chardonnay and Sémillon, and recently started making blanc de blancs, a *méthode champenoise* sparkling wine. Producing just a few thousand cases annually allows Figgins to have a hand in each step of the vinification process.

The Inn at SageCliffe offers packages that let guests experience winemaking firsthand, joining the crew for harvest and crush tasks during autumn. Not interested in heavy lifting? Other getaways include tutored tastings with food pairings led by Figgins and acclaimed chef Fernando Divina, who oversees the on-site restaurant, Tendrils. Winery and vineyard tours can be scheduled in advance, but the self-guided tour, complete with a detailed three-page pamphlet, is well prepared and informative.

A long roster of Cave B attractions—vinotherapy spa treatments, evening lectures on enology, trail rides on horseback—ensures round-the-clock diversions. Future plans include a hilltop village with additional accommodations, another restaurant and tasting bar, international art exhibits, and more robust and diverse culinary programming and wine education. Still, simple pleasures like stargazing and hiking through canyons remain the primary seductions at this pristine destination. ❧

CAVE B WINERY & THE INN AT SAGECLIFFE // 344 Silica Road N.W., Quincy, WA 98848   77

T 509.785.2283
F 509.785.3502
E info@caveb.com

www.caveb.com

ACCESS
About 2 hours from Seattle. From Interstate 90 east- or westbound, take exit 143. Head north onto Silica Road S.W. and continue 5.5 miles to the Cave B entrance.

Hours open for visits and tasting:
11AM–5:30PM daily, January–March;
11AM–5:30PM Sunday–Thursday and
11AM–7PM Friday–Saturday, April–December.

TASTINGS & TOURS
$5 charge for tasting.

Tours: Complimentary self-guided tours available anytime. Guided tours also available; appointment necessary.

Typical wines offered: Cabernet Sauvignon, Merlot, Cuvee du Soleil (Bordeaux blend), Chardonnay, Sémillon, and blanc de blancs.

Sales of wine-related items.

PICNICS & PROGRAMS
Picnic area open to the public. Picnic ingredients sold in tasting room, including SageCliffe line of gourmet foodstuffs.

Special events: Red Wine and Chocolate Celebration in mid-February; Spring Barrel Tasting the third weekend of May; Autumn Crushfest the first weekend of October; Thanksgiving Barrel Tasting; occasional food and wine seminars.

Wine club.

More than 300,000 people visit Chateau Ste. Michelle each year. They come from the fifty states and forty countries where its wines are sold. Japanese tourists descended in droves when Seattle Mariners right-fielder Ichiro Suzuki became an international baseball sensation in 2001. For many visitors, it is their first encounter with a winery.

You couldn't ask for a more accessible introduction to wine touring. Chateau Ste. Michelle's informative tours, wide range of wines, and delightful gardens—designed by the famed Olmsted family in the early 1900s—make a favorable impression on wine novices and aficionados alike.

Producing more than one million cases annually, Chateau Ste. Michelle is a juggernaut of Washington's wine industry. It was instrumental in elevating the Evergreen State to the number-two position for national production, and it has helped smaller wineries gain recognition. The winery turns out thirty bottlings, including highly regarded wines crafted in partnership with wine-world luminaries. It spread the gospel of varietals that thrive in the Northwest and spurred the sleepy town of Woodinville's ascent as a major gastronomic destination.

The oldest winery in the state, Chateau Ste. Michelle has origins dating to the 1930s, when two wine outfits—National Wine Company and Pomerelle—set up shop in Seattle. The two companies merged in 1954, the same year the new company released its first vinifera varietal, Grenache; the company was later renamed Chateau Ste. Michelle. There were key milestones for the winery in the 1960s and '70s. It planted Riesling in the Yakima Valley (today the varietal accounts for the bulk of Chateau Ste. Michelle's output). Acclaimed winemaker André Tchelistcheff, retired from Napa Valley's Beaulieu Vineyards, signed on as a consultant. And in 1974, the *Los Angeles Times* ranked Ste. Michelle's Riesling first in a blind tasting of nineteen Rieslings, bringing the winery to the attention of wine enthusiasts across the country.

In 1976, Chateau Ste. Michelle opened to the public in a grand facility built on the former summer estate of lumber magnate Frederick Stimson. Located about twenty minutes north of Seattle amid old dairy farmland that has since given way to truck farms, wineries, and commerce, burgeoning Woodinville still feels well removed from the fray. At Chateau Ste. Michelle, old-growth firs dwarf the sizeable winery, a rolling lawn accommodates forty-three hundred concertgoers in summer, and the historic Stimson family home is used for special events.

Enjoying such close proximity to Seattle, the winery is equipped to handle a crush of visitors, offering tours every half-hour or hour, depending on the season. The standard thirty-five-minute tour details the château's beginnings but also emphasizes the growing conditions of the Columbia Valley—located a few hours east—where Chateau Ste. Michelle owns thirty-four hundred acres and contracts grapes from other vineyards. The winery refers to its Cold Creek and Canoe Ridge vineyards as green patches in the sunny Yakima desert. Planted during 1972–1973, Cold Creek comprises some of the oldest vines in Washington, and Canoe Ridge is now the site of Chateau Ste. Michelle's red winemaking operation.

The château lobby opens onto a gallery overlooking stabilizing tanks and a Willy Wonka–esque bottling line. A network of catwalks allows visitors to view the inner workings of a large-scale winery while safely

---

CHATEAU STE. MICHELLE VINEYARDS & WINERY // 1 Stimson Lane, P.O. Box 1976, Woodinville, WA 98072

T 800.267.6793; 425.488.1133
F 425.415.3657
E info@ste-michelle.com

www.ste-michelle.com

ACCESS
About 15 miles north of Seattle. From Interstate 405, take exit 23 toward Monroe/Wenatchee. Continue on Highway 522 to the first Woodinville exit. Turn right at the stop and continue to N.E. 175th Street. Turn right, crossing railroad tracks. Turn left at the stop and follow Highway 202, which becomes N.E. 145th Street, approximately 2 miles to the winery.

Hours open for visits and tasting: 10AM–5PM daily, except New Year's Day, Easter, Thanksgiving, and Christmas.

TASTINGS & TOURS
Columbia Valley Tour and Tasting includes complimentary tasting. Premium Wine Tasting is $5 for four reserve and single-vineyard wines. Vintage Reserve Room Tasting is hosted, allowing guests to choose four reserve or single-vineyard samples for $8; reservations required. Ultimate Wine Tasting features food and wine pairings, selected by a winery specialist, for $45; reservations required. No appointment necessary, except as noted above.

Tours: 10:30AM–4:30PM daily. No appointment necessary.

Typical wines offered: Riesling, Chardonnay, Sauvignon Blanc, Sémillon, Pinot Gris, Sauvignon Blanc, Gewürztraminer, Cabernet Sauvignon, Merlot, Syrah, Meritage, and Col Solare (Bordeaux blend).

Sales of wine-related items.

PICNICS & PROGRAMS
Picnic area open to the public. Picnic ingredients sold in tasting room, including assorted cheeses, crackers, and chocolates.

Special events: A dozen summer concerts featuring major touring acts held outdoors; regularly scheduled Wine 101 seminars, wine and cheese–tasting evenings, handicrafts classes, cooking classes, and winemaker's dinners conducted by culinary director John Sarich; Passport to Woodinville open house the first weekend of April; Chateau Ste. Michelle Festival of the Grape in September; St. Nicholas Day open house the first weekend of December.

Wine club.

---

traversing the production facility. Educational posters are hung throughout, denoting Washington appellations, red and white grape varieties, and regional climatic statistics. A patchwork display of awards and honors speaks to Chateau Ste. Michelle's longevity.

One wine that receives many accolades and routinely appears on *The Wine Spectator*'s "Top 100 Wines" list is Eroica Riesling. Chenin Blanc used to be Washington's favored white grape, but Riesling—often crafted in the off-dry style to appeal to Americans' penchant for sweet, sugary drinks—exploded onto the scene in the 1990s. In contrast to floral, melon-rich Rieslings, Eroica is acidic and has a restrained, mineral quality—hallmarks of German Kabinett (dry) Riesling.

In 1999, Chateau Ste. Michelle joined forces with influential German winemaker Dr. Ernst Loosen to craft a Riesling that reflects Columbia Valley soil and the character of the Mosel River (the waterway that cuts through Germany's primary Riesling-growing area). Dr. Loosen works with winemaker Bob Bertheau to choose vineyard plots in the summer, when grapes are ripening, and returns to Washington in December to conduct the final Eroica blending. The partnership is emblematic of other Chateau Ste. Michelle joint ventures, collaborations that enhance the winery's credibility with connoisseurs and provide craft winemakers with spectacular support and resources.

The Artist Series Meritage is another distinctive Chateau Ste. Michelle offering. Beginning in 1996, the winery began commissioning sculptures—initially from revered Washington glass artist Dale Chihuly—to serve as artwork for its Meritage labels. Each vintage features a new label, and many of the abstract works can be seen in the winery's banquet room.

Tours conclude in the busy tasting room with three complimentary wines (guests can taste additional reserve and limited-edition wines for a fee). Guides and staff, some of whom have been with the company for decades, stand out for their knowledge and eagerness to direct visitors to smaller, newer wineries nearby. At its size, Chateau Ste. Michelle can afford to throw the competition a bone. ⁓

Columbia Crest

OWNER: **STE. MICHELLE WINE ESTATES** // WINEMAKER: **RAY EINBERGER**

The largest winery in the Northwest resides in one of Washington's tiniest towns, a hamlet called Paterson that is little more than a windswept intersection with a blinking red light. As you head north from the stoplight, the sun-baked Columbia River Gorge scenery changes, scrub brush and scraggly trees giving way to rows of grapevines as orderly as eighteenth-century marching armies. Beyond acres of vines, a pair of ornate gates interrupts the tidy lines, marking a grand entrance to the winery.

Columbia Crest is modeled after the French châteaux of Bordeaux and Burgundy, and the final construction cost reached twenty-six million dollars at its completion in 1983. It succeeds in evoking an Old World splendor, which is somewhat shocking in these parts but an undeniable draw for visitors. Lush landscaping includes a sizeable manmade pond, rose garden, and flagged patio, but the most impressive sight is a pair of 800,000-gallon blending tanks as big as the nuclear reactor towers farther east in Hanford. You won't find equipment of this ilk at any other winery in the region.

These outdoor tanks, along with smaller 150,000- and 300,000-gallon tanks in the subterranean winemaking facility, allow Columbia Crest to stock supermarket shelves with its bottles of Merlot and Chardonnay in all fifty states and more than thirty countries. The massive scale of the winery also makes possible value pricing that doesn't exceed fifteen dollars a bottle—except for Reserve selections, premium wines in the thirty-dollar neighborhood that receive attentive care and are made to age. While some enthusiasts prefer the character that shines through in handcrafted wines from boutique wineries, Columbia Crest's varietals are consistently praised for offering quality at an accessible price.

Guided tours, offered on weekends, cover much historical and physical ground, lasting thirty to forty-five minutes and traversing a fair swath of the twenty-acre winery, so pack comfy shoes. (During the week, visitors can embark on self-guided tours, making stops in the vineyard, the barrel room, and, of course, the tasting room.) The sumptuous lobby, virtually unchanged since its creation, is a fine place to get your bearings. Guides share the origins of its artisanal materials, which infuse the room with a regal but comfortable air. Chandeliers and sconces are from Spain. The floor tile hails from Italy. French and Belgian fabrics commingle with antique English furniture, and French reproduction tapestries decorate the walls. The colorful volcanic rock framing the fireplace and entryway comes from Baker County, Oregon, and contains natural fossils. In summer, the gallery provides cool relief from the blazing sun, and in winter, an inviting fire blazes indoors.

This is where you'll receive an abbreviated history of Columbia Crest, which was initially named River Ridge and was then, as now, a subsidiary of Ste. Michelle Wine Estates. Vineyard planting in the Horse Heaven Hills commenced in 1978 and continued until 1981, adding five hundred acres each year. (Twenty-five hundred of the property's ten thousand acres are now productive vineyard land.) A Seattle architect designed the estate, which was partially functional by harvest time in 1982 and fully operational and open to the public the following summer. Columbia Crest has mirrored American winemaking trends, producing Riesling, Grenache-based Blush, Cabernet Sauvignon, and

---

COLUMBIA CREST // Highway 221, Columbia Crest Drive, P.O. Box 231, Paterson, WA 99345

T 509.875.2061
F 509.875.2568
E info@columbia-crest.com

www.columbia-crest.com

ACCESS
About 26 miles south of Prosser. From Interstate 84 eastbound, take the Biggs Junction exit and head north over the Columbia River on Highway 97. Turn right on Highway 14 and continue to its intersection with Highway 221. From Interstate 84 westbound, exit at Hermiston/Umitilla onto Interstate 82 and continue until you reach Highway 14. Go west on Highway 14 for 12 miles until it intersects with Highway 221. Proceed north on Highway 221 for 1.5 miles; the winery is to the left.

Hours open for visits and tasting:
10AM–4:30PM daily, except major holidays.

TASTINGS & TOURS
Complimentary tasting of Two Vines and Grand Estates wines. $5 reserve tasting.

Tours: Guided winery tours at 11AM and 1, 2:30, and 4PM, weekends only. Self-guided tours available anytime. No appointment necessary.

Typical wines offered: Chardonnay, Riesling, Gewürztraminer, Sauvignon Blanc, Sémillon, Sémillon-Chardonnay, Cabernet Sauvignon, Merlot, Merlot-Cabernet, Syrah, Walter Clore Private Reserve (proprietary Bordeaux blend), Sémillon Ice Wine, late-harvest Sémillon.

Sales of wine-related items.

PICNICS & PROGRAMS
Picnic area open to the public on the patio and lawns. Picnic ingredients sold in tasting room, including assorted cheeses, deli meats, and crackers.

Special events: Red Wine and Chocolate Celebration in mid-February; Annual April Kite Festival; Spring Barrel Tasting; Catch the Crush fall harvest celebration; Annual Vintage Mustang Car Show in October; Thanksgiving in Wine Country. Other seasonal events include vineyard tours, craft workshops, and special tastings.

Wine club.

Merlot early on and progressively focusing on a few Bordeaux-style blends and varietals such as Syrah and Sauvignon Blanc. Its size permits much experimentation: Columbia Crest produced the country's first Sémillon-Chardonnay blend in 1990, and today winemaker Ray Einberger continues to play, testing varietals and blends in small lots that are sometimes available to try in the tasting room.

The production facility is housed underground to maintain consistent temperature and humidity regardless of vividly hot summers and below-freezing winters. It is a maze of stainless-steel vats, piping, and barrels, entertaining enough to capture kids' interest for at least a little while. Miles of steel pipe wend through the winery, transporting wine from one station to the next in a well-oiled system that strikingly contrasts with the hoist-and-dump procedure at small wineries. A serpentine bottling line handles four hundred bottles per minute, pumps moving furiously to force air into bottles to clear any debris, blast in nitrogen to remove oxygen, and seal the vessels with cork. A display case near the line illustrates how Columbia Crest labels and bottles have evolved.

Columbia Crest is a popular destination, but thanks to its remote location, the winery isn't inundated with crowds, attracting approximately fifty visitors on weekdays and two hundred guests on big days. It's a gratifying surprise to receive one-on-one attention at such a huge place, and spending some time at ground zero for one of the United States' most visible wine labels gives you context for Washington's wine industry as a whole. It's not at all what you would expect from a winery that produces some two million cases annually. ✑

Columbia Winery

Columbia Winery has seen its share of changes since it incorporated in 1962. Reflecting the growing pains and triumphs that the Washington wine industry as a whole has experienced, the winery experimented with different vineyards and grape varieties, suffered criticisms of unstructured, indistinct wines, and felt the groundswell of enthusiasm for Riesling and Syrah. It has changed names, moved four times, and enjoyed exponential growth. One force that has remained constant for over twenty-five years is winemaker David Lake, who continues to define, challenge, and refine Columbia Winery's gestalt.

Columbia is a short drive from Seattle, located in pastoral Woodinville across the street from the well-known winery Chateau Ste. Michelle. Second in longevity to its larger neighbor, Columbia dates to 1956, when two University of Washington doctors began making wine at home. In 1962, the amateur group expanded to include ten friends, six of whom were Husky professors, and together they formed Associated Vintners. They placed faith where few others dared, staking their venture on the conviction that Old World vinifera vines could flourish in the northerly Evergreen State.

The group planted vineyards and reaped good results in the late 1960s. In 1976, the winery moved to Redmond, south of Seattle, and produced wine on a sizeable scale. Lake joined as enologist three years later, quickly becoming winemaker, a role that would allow him to make crucial advances at Columbia over three decades.

Lake became a Master of Wine in 1975 and spent a few years working with vintners in California and Oregon before moving northward. He is credited with a handful of notable Washington firsts. Recognizing the distinctive qualities of grapes from individual plots, in 1981 he was the first to release wines designated by single vineyards. In 1988, he produced the premiere Washington Syrah; three years later, Lake made the state's first Cabernet Franc. In 1994, he ushered in Pinot Gris. Lake is also among a group of pioneering winemakers to experiment with Viognier and Mourvèdre, a late-ripening red grape important in southern Spain and Provence.

Lake's close, collaborative relationships with growers have fostered many of his winemaking initiatives. Columbia Winery doesn't own vineyards, but it maintains long-term contracts, some exclusive, with renowned vineyards in the Columbia Valley. Columbia's partnership with Red Willow Vineyard—the northernmost and highest planting in the Yakima Valley appellation—is crucial. Lake started working with Red Willow owner Mike Sauer in his first year at Columbia, and together they pioneered a signature series of Cabernet Sauvignon, Syrah, and Cabernet Franc. Sauer manages his vineyard according to slope angle, sun exposure, and soil type, demarcating twenty-seven discrete blocks among six varietals. Once mature, each block of grapes is harvested and vinified separately, allowing Lake to work with isolated flavor and aroma characteristics to craft single-origin or blended varietals.

Columbia Winery visitors may be more interested in sipping and shopping than in dissecting the intricacies of winemaking. More than 300,000 people visit the winery annually, two-thirds of whom arrive via dinner train from Renton. The *Spirit of Washington* is a vintage train that takes passengers on a three-hour journey along the east side of Lake Washington, serving

---

COLUMBIA WINERY // 14030 N.E. 145th Street, P.O. Box 1248, Woodinville, WA 98072

T 800.488.2347; 425.488.2776
F 425.488.3460
E contact@columbiawinery.com

www.columbiawinery.com

ACCESS
About 15 miles north of Seattle. From Interstate 405, take exit 23 toward Monroe/Wenatchee. Follow Highway 522 to the first Woodinville exit. Turn right at the stop and continue to N.E. 175th Street. Turn right, crossing railroad tracks. Turn left at the stop and follow Highway 202, which becomes N.E. 145th Street, approximately 2 miles to the winery.

Hours open for visits and tasting:
10AM–6PM daily, except major holidays.

TASTINGS & TOURS
Complimentary tasting of Columbia Winery wines; $5 Signature Series Tasting includes five Reserve wines.

Tours: 3:30PM weekdays and on the hour 11AM–5PM Saturday–Sunday (no 1 or 2PM Saturday; no noon or 1PM Sunday).
No appointment necessary.

Typical wines offered: Barbera, Cabernet Franc, Cabernet Sauvignon, Chardonnay, Gewürztraminer, Merlot, Merlot-Cabernet blend, Pinot Gris, Riesling, Sangiovese, Sémillon, Syrah, Viognier, and Zinfandel.

Sales of wine-related items.

PICNICS & PROGRAMS
Picnic area open to the public. Picnic ingredients sold in tasting room, including sandwiches, assorted cheeses and salamis, and other light snacks.

Special events: March into Spring the first weekend in March; Passport to Woodinville open house the first weekend of April; discounted Case by Case Sale in mid-August; Art of Crush tour during harvest; Taste of Red the second weekend of November; St. Nicholas Day open house the first weekend of December; and frequent cooking classes and wine education classes throughout the year.

Wine club.

---

a three-course meal and pausing at Columbia Winery for a forty-five-minute visit. The train operates year-round, daily during the summer, bringing the winery hordes of visitors. The winery expanded in 1998, unveiling a gargantuan tasting room and shop to accommodate the onslaught of guests.

Today the winery resembles a rambling Cape house, with a large wraparound veranda, peaked turret, and cheerful gardens. Picnic tables arrayed on a pristine lawn beckon, while a large bar inside the shop lets dozens of guests gather around to sample Columbia's wines. Brief tours through parts of the production facility and cellar provide a sound introduction to Columbia's philosophy and wine styles. In keeping with Lake's innovative approach, his team experiments with different yeast strains and lab technologies. When the conglomerate Constellation Brands acquired Columbia in 2001 (Constellation has a large portfolio of wineries including Robert Mondavi, Ravenswood, and Ruffino), it invested in new equipment and bestowed a wealth of resources. It's a happy marriage of corporation and craft.

Though Columbia Winery turns out about 150,000 cases of wine each year, its onsite capacity is 40,000 cases, necessitating the production of Riesling and Gewürztraminer at sister winery Covey Run. Apace with statewide output, Riesling accounts for more than half of Columbia's case yield, and Gewürztraminer is catching up. Like consumer tastes, Columbia's wines continue to evolve, and the winery strives to reintroduce drinkers to its products. As assistant winemaker Robert Takahashi points out, "We're not the same Columbia Winery as ten or fifteen years ago."

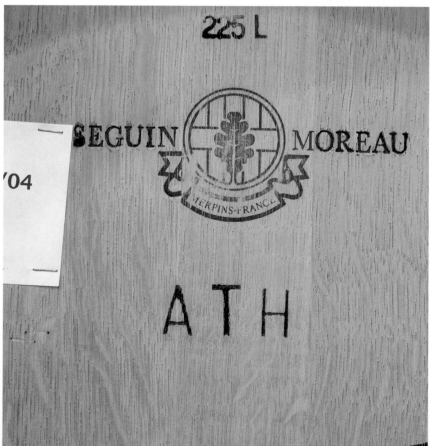

225 L

SEGUIN ◆ MOREAU

MERPINS-FRANCE

'04

ATH

Kestrel Vintners

OWNERS: JOHN & HELEN WALKER // WINEMAKER: FLINT NELSON

During the construction boom of the late 1980s, Miami developer John Walker came to Washington to build a harness-racing track. While planning a course for horse-and-buggy racers, he fell in love with the clean, fruity wines emerging in the state. When it was time to return home, he was infuriated to learn that state laws prohibited shipment of wines from Washington to Florida. Walker devised a solution: he bought a winery. As a winery licensee, he was able to ensure an endless supply of great Washington wines delivered to his home in southern Florida.

It was an extravagant remedy, perhaps, but one that led ultimately to the formation of Kestrel Vintners, a small, quality-oriented winery whose fruits would soon be enjoyed by many others besides Walker and his wife, Helen. He installed winemaker Ray Sandidge with the charge to make fine wines, if not necessarily a fine profit. Kestrel produced its first vintages of Cabernet Sauvignon and Chardonnay in 1995 and opened its Prosser winery and tasting room in February 1999. As Kestrel racked up awards and recognition, Walker issued winery staff new marching orders in 2001: work toward self sufficiency, but keep wine prices affordable.

Kestrel bills itself as a winery with attitude, a Washington State attitude, which presumably means it is laid-back and without pretense. There is no whiff of braggadocio at the tasting room, a humble, inviting bar and shop situated at a crossroads in the Yakima Valley. From the outset, the tasting room has carried a wide selection of artisanal cheeses curated by the Cheesemonger shop in touristy Leavenworth, Washington. Though the assortment is constantly in flux, you can count on outstanding English Cotswold, Drunken Goat, and Stilton to nibble on while you try Kestrel's wines, and you can purchase larger quantities for a picnic on the winery's front lawn.

There are dozens of wineries in the Yakima Valley, Washington's first major concentration of vintners (and the state's first designated appellation), but it is lonesome country, an arid landscape devoid of lush vegetation and large communities. It may look barren, but it is prime grape-growing territory, enjoying intense heat, extended daylight, and cool nights. The region receives little rain during the growing season and benefits from gentle summer winds that mitigate the burn of high daytime temperatures. The Yakima boasts more than ten thousand vineyard acres—second only to Washington's much larger Columbia Valley—that supply grapes to wineries across the Northwest.

Walker had the keen sense to purchase a prime 160-acre plot planted with vines dating to 1972, some of the oldest Chardonnay, Merlot, and Cabernet Sauvignon stock in the state. Kestrel View Estate Vineyard sits at twelve hundred feet, divided into equal north and south blocks, a short drive from the winery.

After years of producing high-end varietals, Kestrel released a wine that struck a nerve with consumers in a way the winery never predicted. In 2001, winemaker Flint Nelson faced a surplus of wine left over from blending with no intended use. Students enrolled in the enology and viticulture program at nearby Columbia Basin Community College adopted Kestrel's dilemma as a class project and came up with a robust red blend and a killer marketing plan. The key was a catchy label that would stand out on bloated grocery store shelves. A fun name didn't hurt, either. And the proposal also granted the winemaker necessary flexibility, allowing for varying percentages of Syrah, Merlot, and Cabernet Sauvignon from bottling to bottling, depending on what Nelson had on his hands.

June 2004 marked the first release of Drop Dead Red, a moderately priced crowd-pleaser featuring a sultry pin-up with a copper mane. Local artist Michael Rostovitch illustrated the Vargas-inspired knockout, using a ceramic-transfer label notable for its texture and vibrant colors. At the time Kestrel was a six-thousand-case winery, but it took a leap of faith and bottled three thousand cases of Drop Dead. It sold out within three months. Subsequent, larger-run editions—each sporting an alluring new label—were snapped up just as quickly. In 2006, Kestrel turned out twelve thousand cases of the wine, renamed Lady in Red due to a naming dispute with an Oregon winery.

The runaway success of Lady in Red propelled Kestrel to financial solvency and spurred the winery to create a second market-driven wine. Platinum is a fifty-fifty blend of Viognier and Gewürztraminer, designed for a sweeter palate and strongly promoted at the winery's satellite tasting room in Leavenworth. Introduced in 2005, Platinum is also on a path to exponential growth.

Crowd-pleasing blends are Kestrel's bread and butter, but they are almost a separate entity. The winery's soul is rooted in premium varietals made with select fruit and aged for eight months to two years in barrels and six months to two years in bottles. Kestrel places special emphasis on crafting wines meant to be cellared and occasionally holds back a portion of a vintage to release years later. In 2005, it unveiled a thousand bottles of 1999 Cabernet Sauvignon as a treat for wine club members and lucky tasting-room visitors. ❧

KESTREL VINTNERS // 2890 Lee Road, Prosser, WA 99350

T 888.343.2675; 509.786.2675
F 509.786.2679
E winery@kestrelwines.com

www.kestrelwines.com

ACCESS
From Interstate 82 east- or westbound, take exit 82 to Prosser. At the stop, turn right onto Wine Country Road. Take the first left, then turn right onto Lee Road. The winery is the third building on the left.

Hours open for visits and tasting:
10AM–5PM daily, except major holidays.

TASTINGS & TOURS
No charge for tasting.

Tours by appointment only.

Typical wines offered: Cabernet Sauvignon, Merlot, Syrah, Sangiovese, Chardonnay, Viognier, Lady in Red (premium red blend), Platinum (Viognier-Gewürztraminer blend).

Sales of wine-related items.

PICNICS & PROGRAMS
Picnic area open to the public. Picnic ingredients sold in tasting room, including a large assortment of imported cheeses and salami. Bistro plates and wines by the glass sold in summer.

Special events: Red Wine and Chocolate Celebration in mid-February; Barrel Tasting in late April; Kestrel Festival in mid-June; Catch the Crush fall harvest celebration in September; Thanksgiving in Wine Country; seasonal winemaker's dinners.

Wine club.

Pacific Northwest : WASHINGTON

Walla Walla's transformation—from a remote agricultural town that only attracted tourists during Parents' Weekend at Whitman College into a wining-and-dining hot spot—can be attributed in part to its wealth of tantalizing stories. The most famous story dates back to 1847, when missionaries Mark and Narcissa Whitman, blamed for an incurable measles outbreak among the Cayuse tribe, were brutally murdered in a camp raid. Eleven other settlers were also killed and sixty taken hostage in what came to be known as the Whitman Massacre, an incident of such magnitude that it precipitated the Cayuse War and the establishment of the Oregon Territory.

The tales circulating today are about wine, not Whitman, and they are redefining the character of this old fur-trapping crossroads. With the number of licensed wineries nearing triple digits, Walla Walla has earned its own appellation and boasts a remarkably collaborative industry, with wineries trading expertise, equipment, and all manner of hands-on help.

"When I joined L'Ecole in 1989, there were six or seven wineries, and we were clearly trying to put Washington on the world wine stage," says winemaker and co-owner Marty Clubb. "Now we're recognized as a quality winemaking region. Our focus is conveying what it is that makes Walla Walla wines unique. But we all owe a lot to Rick Small of Woodward Canyon and Gary Figgins of Leonetti Cellar—they really drove the push for quality and set the standard."

When you're talking stories, few Walla Walla wineries have as many to tell as L'Ecole Nº 41. Local luminaries Baker and Jean Ferguson began renovating the shuttered, vacant Lowden elementary school (formerly district Nº 41) in 1979, diving into the winemaking business as a retirement project. It wasn't the first occupational twist for Walla Walla native Baker, who served as an Air Force B-17 navigator during World War II (and was held as a prisoner of war for two years), taught economics and business administration at Whitman College, and eventually become president of the historic Baker Boyer Bank in downtown Walla Walla.

Baker didn't have much winemaking experience, but he was a serious oenophile and counted pioneering Leonetti winemaker Figgins among his close friends. From the start, L'Ecole Nº 41 focused on crafting the premium Bordeaux varietals Merlot and Sémillon, a silky white that has recently come into vogue but was virtually unknown in the Northwest when L'Ecole released its inaugural 1983 vintage. The winery quickly racked up accolades—including a gold for its first Merlot from the Washington Enological Society—while the Fergusons, who hadn't anticipated such furious demand, started losing steam. Enter their daughter, Megan Clubb, and her husband, Marty. For the Fergusons, selling L'Ecole to the Clubbs was a surefire way to lure them from San Francisco back to Walla Walla while ensuring L'Ecole's continued existence as a small, family-run winery emphasizing handcrafted wines.

Family ephemera is everywhere at the winsome schoolhouse winery, whose charm has aided the brand's success. Situated just outside Walla Walla, next to renowned winery Woodward Canyon, the winery derives its name from the 1915 Craftsman schoolhouse it inhabits. The Fergusons added a second story, which initially served as their residence so they could be close to the all-consuming business; the elaborate stairway (and glass-paneled bookcases in the tasting room) came from Stubblefield Mansion, Baker Ferguson's family home. These are just a couple of the many intriguing details lurking at L'Ecole. In the tasting room, you'll notice an unusual chunky table, a checkwriting stand that originally resided in Baker Boyer Bank and then served as the initial tasting bar during the winery's early days. A sleek clock from the bank hangs on the wall over cases holding gourmet vinegars, bright aprons, and souvenir T-shirts.

And there are many remnants of the school itself: a flagpole out front, a playground in the back, a small coal-storage nook rechristened as a detention room to discourage unruly behavior among winery guests, classic pendant lamps, chalkboards (plus a new slate-topped bar for customer doodling), and a Lilliputian-sized drinking fountain. The indoor recess room in the basement has been converted to barrel storage, and the boys' and girls' washrooms are still employed as restrooms.

Hitting the market with a thousand cases of the 1983 vintage, L'Ecole steadily increased production each year and now holds steady at an annual output of thirty thousand cases, an amount that allows Clubb to personally oversee its vineyards. Clubb cites vigilant vineyard management as the most important improvement in L'Ecole's wines in recent years. And the winery has some choice sites, including acreage at revered Pepper Bridge and Seven Hills vineyards. L'Ecole also has land in the Columbia Valley, ensuring it will have fruit even if a frost sabotages its Walla Walla vines, which happens about every seven years.

For a relatively small winery, the brand enjoys excellent placement in restaurants and key retailers, with distribution in forty-eight states. But as thousands of new visitors flocking to this revived boomtown have discovered, sampling L'Ecole wines at the winery is still a singular experience. ✍

86

L'ECOLE Nº 41 // 41 Lowden School Road, P.O. Box 111, Lowden, WA 99360

T 509.525.0940
F 509.525.2775
E info@lecole.com

www.lecole.com

ACCESS
About 13 miles west of Walla Walla. From Walla Walla, take Highway 12 west to Dry Creek Road. From points west, take Route 12 east to Dry Creek Road. Turn north onto Dry Creek Road, then left into the winery parking lot.

Hours open for visits and tasting:
10AM–5PM daily, except major holidays.

TASTINGS & TOURS
No charge for tasting. $3 per-person fee for groups of ten or larger; must be arranged in advance.

Tours: No tours.

Typical wines offered: Sémillon, Chardonnay, Chenin Blanc, Merlot, Cabernet Sauvignon, Syrah, Recess Red (proprietary blend), Apogee, and Perigee (Bordeaux-style blends).

Sales of wine-related items.

PICNICS & PROGRAMS
Picnic area open to the public by the old school playground behind the winery and near the demonstration vineyard in front. No picnic ingredients sold in tasting room.

Special events: Spring Release Weekend the first weekend of May; Vintage Walla Walla the first weekend of June; Holiday Barrel Tasting the first weekend of December.

Wine club.

Maryhill Winery

OWNERS: CRAIG & VICKI LEUTHOLD, DON LEUTHOLD & CHERIE BROOKS // WINEMAKER: JOHN HAW

Facing stiff competition from snow-capped volcanoes, the brash Oregon coastline, and captivating high-desert plateaus, the Columbia River Gorge is nevertheless one of the most spectacular natural features in the Northwest. Petroglyph etchings and centuries-old stories bear testament to beliefs held by Native Americans, explorers, and early settlers that this endures as a sacred place. As you pass through the gorge, you glimpse seasonal waterfalls where you never saw them before and notice how the shifting daylight colors the rock cliffs. Situated on a bluff, Maryhill Winery enjoys an enviable vantage over this chameleon landscape.

Many travelers discover Maryhill Winery en route to other destinations in the gorge—an afternoon at the quirky Maryhill Museum, lunch in Hood River, a hike on a segment of the Pacific Coast Trail. They turn off at Goldendale out of curiosity, intending to stop in for a quick taste. Four hours later they are still there, installed on the winery's vine-covered patio with a nice Sangiovese Rosé. The gorge has a way of rendering the passing of time irrelevant.

Maryhill co-owners Craig and Vicki Leuthold experienced the pull of the gorge again and again on trips down from Spokane. When they began to consider opening a winery, they realized the physical attributes that made the area so magical also made it extremely well suited to growing grapes. "Nowhere else in the world is there this mountain range that blocks the rain and this great river that acts as a gigantic heat sink," Craig explains. "Cool nights and hot days produce high acidity in the grapes. The only thing we have to worry about is the Northern Express—losing grapes to an early frost."

In 1997, the Leutholds got their feet wet by investing in nearby Cascade Cliffs Vineyard & Winery. Through Cascade Cliffs, they met brothers Dan and Ron Gunkel, fourth-generation farmers who had been growing grapes and stone fruit in the area. In a lucky twist, the Gunkels were selling a tract of vineyard-designated land. The Leutholds bought the property, and today the Gunkels manage Maryhill's vineyards.

Affable and easy-going, with their lovable, galumphing Great Pyrenees, Potter, at their side, the Leutholds don't come across as hard-nosed business-people, but in just a few years they built Maryhill into a hugely successful venture. Their philosophy is simple: give people what they want. "We are absolutely a market-driven winery," Craig says. "We make thirteen varietals and have every desire to accommodate changing tastes and trends." Maryhill produced its 1999 and 2000 vintages at Washington's Hogue Cellars before completing construction of the winery in summer 2001. The operation was profitable within three years, and annual production rocketed from four thousand to forty thousand cases in six years. Craig says it could grow to sixty thousand cases in another couple of years.

For his part, winemaker John Haw, formerly of Sokol Blosser Winery, wants Maryhill to showcase what Washington can do, experimenting with various grapes and wine styles to test the capabilities of the land. Maryhill emphasizes premium reds, especially Sangiovese and Syrah, but also produces large quantities of Zinfandel, Cabernet Sauvignon, Merlot, and Viognier. Smaller plots are given over to less proven varietals, including Grenache, Malbec, and Cabernet Franc.

In the south-facing tasting room and shop, wines are displayed in wooden crates and identified with descriptive tags listing details such as fruit source, bottling date, residual sugar level, and number of cases produced. Rivaling the view, an elaborately carved antique bar anchors the tasting area. Made of extinct quarter-sawn tiger oak, the beautiful piece originated in Germany and traveled around Cape Horn to Juneau during the Klondike Gold Rush of the late 1890s. When winter winds make lounging on the patio out of the question, guests congregate around the striking bar and by the stone fireplace, where they can leaf through a compelling selection of wine books and magazines.

The three-story winery is modest, designed to accentuate, not overpower, the striking scenery. The Leutholds knew they'd be spending most of their time tending to business in the early years, so the plans included a residence on the top floor, which will be converted to event use when round-the-clock demands ease. Maryhill already hosts a variety of celebrations, including major concerts in its large amphitheater. The location makes it a natural choice for live music, and the Leutholds felt that concerts would be a great way for people to become acquainted with Maryhill's wines—and remember them when confronted with hundreds of other choices at the grocery store. With annual visitation to the winery up to seventy-five thousand and growing, word of Maryhill's many attractions is clearly making the rounds. ☙

MARYHILL WINERY // 9774 Highway 14, Goldendale, WA 98620

T 877.627.9445
F 509.773.0586
E info@maryhillwinery.com

www.maryhillwinery.com

ACCESS
From Interstate 84 east- or westbound, take the Biggs Junction exit to the north. Head north on Route 97 until it intersects with Highway 14. Take Highway 14 west for about 5 miles. The winery is on the left, just past the Maryhill Museum.

Hours open for visits and tasting: 10AM–6PM daily, except major holidays.

TASTINGS & TOURS
Complimentary tasting of premium wines, $5 to taste five Reserve wines.

Tours: By appointment only.

Typical wines offered: Sangiovese, Syrah, Zinfandel, Cabernet Sauvignon, Grenache, Malbec, Cabernet Franc, Chardonnay, Sauvignon Blanc, Riesling, Gewürztraminer, Pinot Gris, and Viognier.

Sales of wine-related items.

PICNICS & PROGRAMS
Picnic area open to the public on the patio and amphitheater. Picnic ingredients sold in tasting room, including preserved meats, assorted cheeses, spreads, and a variety of crackers.

Special events: Several summer concerts featuring major touring acts in the amphitheater; many holiday weekend events, including Valentine's Day Chocolate and Red Wine Festival; Spring Release Party; Memorial Weekend Anniversary Party; Annual Peach Harvest; Labor Day Barbecue; and Harvest Celebration.

Wine club.

Some people go to wineries to learn about wine. Some people go to relax. And some go to…play a few holes of golf? Well, visitors to Three Rivers Winery in Walla Walla have that option.

A trio of couples joined forces in the late 1990s to create a first for Walla Walla: a destination winery. Established in 1998, Three Rivers was the fourteenth licensed winery to emerge in the burgeoning scene. The partners—all with business backgrounds, and two of whom worked together in cellular communications— saw the potential for growth in the small Eastern Washington community.

Thanks to early pioneers Leonetti Cellar and Woodward Canyon, Walla Walla earned a reputation for exceptional wines. Other small operations followed suit, and the local wine industry gained momentum during the Internet boom years of the mid- to late '90s. Wine enthusiasts and tourists began trickling in, drawn by the quality wines and downtown Walla Walla's turn-of-the-century charm.

Partners Steve Ahler, Charles Stocking III, and Duane Wollmuth saw a niche in providing visitors with a complete wine country experience from vine to wine. "We wanted to create a facility where people could immerse themselves in the experience—see the vines growing in the vineyard, see wine being made in the production facility, taste the wines and buy gifts in the tasting room, and relax with a picnic on the deck," Wollmuth says.

To that end, Three Rivers encompasses a four-thousand-square-foot tasting room well stocked with gifts, T-shirts, books, and gourmet packaged foods. On one side of the large open room, an expansive window provides a glimpse of the production area, awash in shiny stainless steel. The opposite side offers a very different view, one that encourages guests to idle on the deck for hours. The distant Blue Mountains are a vivid backdrop for the small vineyard and subtly landscaped three-hole golf course. "The guys over at Woodward Canyon and L'Ecole No 41 were always hitting balls into the fields behind them," Wollmuth says, referring to two nearby wineries. "We had three acres that were too low for vines that needed to be landscaped, so we decided to put in three holes and landscape around that." He jokes that the grand plan was for the other wineries to each add a miniature golf course so they could hold round-robin tournaments.

Although the links and leisurely picnics beckon in mild weather, visitors can amuse themselves indoors as well, snuggling into leather chairs in front of the river rock fireplace and perusing the collection of wine magazines. Exposed beams and a vaulted ceiling lend a rustic feel, while the polished stone tasting bar would be at home in a sleek modern kitchen. A spacious banquet room accommodates corporate retreats, private events, and winemaker's dinners.

In 2003, one of these dinners initiated a coup for Walla Walla. Three Rivers invited Mike Davis, then executive chef at the Salish Lodge & Spa near Seattle, to craft a meal that would harmonize with the winery's spring release selections. Davis was taken with the passionate wine scene and small-town goodwill of Walla Walla. He and his family moved to town and opened 26brix Restaurant the following year. It is now Walla Walla's most talked-about restaurant, which is high praise in a town boasting more than its share of excellent eateries.

The current of camaraderie running through Walla Walla is hard to miss. "There's a strong sense of community here, and we all want to see each other thrive," Wollmuth says. He recounts a brainstorming meeting with Norm McKibben, of the renowned Pepper Bridge Vineyard and Winery, and Woodward Canyon founder Rick Small. "They reviewed our business plan, gave us feedback, really helped us out. They realize that if one winery succeeds, we all succeed."

While Three Rivers caters to consumers with some nice amenities, making premium wine is the first priority. Winemaker Holly Turner put in time at Chateau Ste. Michelle and at Bodega la Rural Winery in Argentina before signing on at Three Rivers. The winery grows about 30 percent of its own fruit, contracting grapes from various Columbia Valley vineyards. Because growing conditions in Washington yield a wide range of varietals, Turner gets to flex her muscles in producing a diverse portfolio of wines, ranging from a white Meritage to a late-harvest Gewürztraminer. Producing thirteen thousand to fifteen thousand cases annually, Three Rivers serves market niches by making small quantities of several wines instead of large amounts of just a few varieties.

Three Rivers gives customers an incentive to try new wines by promoting a different wine each month and offering a 15 percent discount on sales. This is a wise tactic that keeps locals coming back to the tasting room on a regular basis, a connection that the winery especially values. "Of all the accolades and favorable ratings we've received, we take most pride in being voted best local winery in a reader survey in the *Walla Walla Union-Bulletin* for two years straight," Wollmuth says. "That means we've succeeded in establishing ourselves in the community, and locals are our best spokespeople—they tell visitors where to go."

THREE RIVERS WINERY // 5641 W. Highway 12, P.O. Box 402, Walla Walla, WA 99362

T 509.526.9463
F 509.529.3436
E info@threeriverswinery.com

www.threeriverswinery.com

ACCESS
About 6 miles west of Walla Walla. From Walla Walla, head east on Highway 12; the winery is on the south side of the highway. From Pasco and the Tri-Cities, head east on Highway 12 for approximately 40 miles.

Hours open for visits and tasting: 10AM–6PM daily, except Thanksgiving Day, Christmas Day, and New Year's Day.

TASTINGS & TOURS
Complimentary tasting of Columbia Valley-series wines. $5 to taste vineyard-designated and reserve wines.

Tours: Appointment recommended.

Typical wines offered: Chardonnay, Meritage White, Cabernet Sauvignon, Meritage Red, rosé, red table wine, Sangiovese, Syrah, and late-harvest Gewürztraminer.

Sales of wine-related items.

PICNICS & PROGRAMS
Picnic area open to the public on the deck. Picnic ingredients sold in tasting room, including cheeses, crackers, olives, and chocolates.

Special events: Spring Release the first weekend in May; Balloon Stampede Weekend in mid-May; Vintage Walla Walla in early June; Holiday Barrel Tasting the first weekend in December; seasonal winemaker's dinners.

Wine club.

For decades, the hills rising up from Lake Chelan were covered with gnarled apple trees. Before organic farming went mainstream, before New Zealand and Chile began cultivating crisp, tart apple varieties, before consumers were given alternatives to the picture-perfect but oversweet and mealy Red Delicious, the ubiquitous apple was Washington's big cash crop.

In the 1980s, Red Delicious represented three-quarters of the Evergreen State's apple harvest. But by 2003, its share had shrunk to one-third. The summer resort community of Chelan, apple industry epicenter and onetime Red Delicious Capital of the World, had settled into an economic slump.

Dr. Bob Jankelson, a dentistry innovator and teacher who retired from Seattle to Chelan in 1994, believed the way to revive Chelan's rich agricultural tradition was to turn fallow orchards into productive vineyards. Jankelson's teaching stints took him to Italy dozens of times during his career, and he fell hard for the "art of Italian living." He was besotted with Italy's slower pace, art and architecture, beautiful countryside, and, most of all, wines. He decided to take a chance on Chelan's soils and slopes by planting vines and building Tsillan Cellars, a showstopper of a winery. Jankelson broke ground on the 135-acre property in February 2003, hoping that other wineries would follow his lead.

By 2006, a dozen wineries ringed alligator-shaped Lake Chelan. Tender vines sprouted on old orchard land, and the region earned recognition as a sub-appellation. In just a couple of years, Chelan was on the rebound, drawing tourists not just for lakeside recreation, but also for its eclectic grassroots winery scene.

As scenic destinations go, Chelan is hard to beat. Nestled at the southeastern tip of the lake, the town of thirty-five hundred boasts a pedestrian-friendly main street cluttered with inviting shops and restaurants. Sunshine reigns in these high-desert plains, safely in the rain shadow of the Cascade Range. Freshly constructed wineries hug the north and south shores of Lake Chelan, a captivating body of water that is the third deepest freshwater lake in the country.

Tsillan Cellars takes its name from a native term that means "deep water." But the winery owes more to Italian culture than to any other. With the help of an interior designer and contractor, Jankelson designed the winery to resemble an Italian country estate. "I was committed to avoiding faux-anything," Jankelson says. "I wanted to use only natural materials." Though Tsillan Cellars doesn't hew to one period or region, it handsomely blends Italian architectural details.

The large umber structure is supported by tumbled marble columns and hand-joined beams weighing 8,700 pounds each. Accented by heavy custom ironwork, the massive beams are exposed in the tasting room: glance upward and you'll notice small white crystals encasing the wood. They are salt crystals, residue from the timbers' earlier life as a turn-of-the-century railroad trestle spanning the Great Salt Lake. The floor is Italian porcelain with inlaid mosaics; travertine stone composes pillars and walls. The tasting bar is slab marble, and even the restrooms—complete with bronze murals and decorative tile—evoke elegance.

Boasting a terrific view of the lake, the grounds are equally attractive. An intricate water feature forms the focal point of the slate patio and cleverly includes an islandlike stage for summer concerts. Jankelson plotted a grand, amenity-rich destination winery to jumpstart agritourism in Chelan, and now Tsillan Cellars sees about five hundred visitors daily during the summer. Though he plans to grow the business, he prefers to focus on the winery site rather than putting effort into gaining wide distribution of Tsillan wines. "Ultimately, 85 percent of our production will be sold out of the tasting room." Tsillan currently produces about eight thousand cases per year, nearly half of which is made with estate fruit from forty (and counting) planted acres.

Winemaker Peter Devison and consulting winemaker Brian Carter have found that the growing conditions that yielded ripe, juicy apples also generate ripe, concentrated grapes. Cold air drops off vineyard slopes, absorbed by Lake Chelan, and the lake contributes regulated airflow, mitigating the need for wind machines. Temperatures plummet in winter, but they don't fluctuate dramatically, allowing vines to cease sap production before frost rolls in. (Killing frosts occur when vines are still active and filled with sap.)

TSILLAN CELLARS // 3875 Highway 97-A, P.O. Box 1759, Chelan, WA 98816

T 877.682.8463; 509.682.9463
F 509.682.2999
E info@tsillancellarswines.com

www.tsillancellarswines.com

ACCESS
About 3 hours from Seattle. From Seattle, take I-90 east to exit 85. Turn left onto Highway 970E and proceed 35 miles over Blewett Pass to Highway 2. Turn right and follow it approximately 15 miles to Wenatchee. Take Highway 97-A toward Entiat/Chelan and proceed 33 miles north to Chelan. Travel through the town and toward the south shore of Lake Chelan. The winery is on the right.

Hours open for visits and tasting:
11AM–5PM daily in winter; 11AM–7PM daily in summer. Closed major holidays and the first week of January.

TASTINGS & TOURS
No charge for tasting.

Tours: 1 and 3PM daily April through October. No appointment necessary.

Typical wines offered: Chardonnay, Riesling, Gewürztraminer, Viognier, Cabernet Franc Rosé, Cabernet Franc, Cabernet Sauvignon, Sangiovese, Merlot, and Bellissima Rossa (Bordeaux blend).

Sales of wine-related items.

PICNICS & PROGRAMS
Picnic area open to the public on the patio. Picnic ingredients sold in tasting room, including salami, prosciutto, smoked salmon, a variety of cheeses, crackers, fresh fruit, olives, nuts, and spreads.

Special events: Lake Chelan Winterfest in mid-January; Red Wine and Chocolate celebration in mid-February; Spring Barrel Tasting; Chelan Nouveau new release weekend in April; Lake Chelan Fall Wine Festival in September; October Crush Festival; Fall Barrel Tasting in November; Lake Chelan Holiday Lighting Tour in December; concerts throughout the summer featuring major touring acts.

Wine club.

Carter and Devison discovered that white varietals—including Riesling, Gewürztraminer, Pinot Grigio, and Chardonnay—shine in this climate. They are betting that popular Syrah will flourish, and they are experimenting with a small Italian vineyard planted with Sangiovese, Nebbiolo, and Barbera. Devison finds Chelan's conditions similar to those of Mendoza, Argentina, and he believes that Malbec will also thrive.

Jankelson and Devison, full of vigor and optimism, epitomize the pioneering attitude of winegrowers in Chelan. Jankelson recognizes the region is young and inexperienced and knows success relies in part on Chelan's ability to promote and differentiate itself. But Jankelson has a few ideas up his sleeve. "My ultimate wish is to build Tsillan out as a complete resort with a spa, villas, and an Italian marketplace," he explains. That's quite a leap from roadside apple stands. ❦

Unpleasant experiences with belittling waiters and snobbish sommeliers give wine a bad rap. These run-ins foster the notion that wine is like skeet shooting and falconry—a pursuit of the elite—and you'd better keep your mouth shut if you don't know your Merlot from your Mourvèdre.

But spend some time talking with winemakers, the artisans of the industry, and you'll notice a common modest refrain. Far from unfurling their credentials and waxing lyrical about the art of crafting a perfect Pinot Noir, most winemakers defer to the grape. Making wine is easy, the mantra goes, if you start with good fruit. But you can't make great wine from mediocre grapes.

Greatly downplaying his skill, Joel Goodwillie would have you believe that few things are simpler than making wine. He and his wife, Kris Goodwillie, bottled their first Wind River Cellars vintage in 1995. Joel didn't enroll in classes at UC Davis, or apprentice at a venerable winery. He simply took a job with Hood River Vineyards, working one harvest, and relied upon the expertise of friends in the industry. "It was much more important to learn the business side of running a winery," he says. "I knew I could figure out how to make wine, but I'm glad I learned how to sell it."

Joel's first job out of college was in sales and marketing at the colossal E. & J. Gallo Winery, a decision he says was born out of "poverty," not a passion for wine. One of the wineries Goodwillie represented during his three years at Gallo was southern Oregon's Callahan Ridge. When the winery went up for sale, Goodwillie struck a deal with the owners, convincing them to keep it if he succeeded in increasing its sales. He and Kris, who met as students at Eastern Washington University, married at Callahan Ridge and became partners in the winery. Kris managed the tasting room, raising Callahan's profile by staging creative events, while Joel spurred sales to unprecedented heights. After five years and an unsuccessful bid to buy out the majority owners, the Goodwillies left to start a winery of their own.

Former windsurfers, the Goodwillies knew the charms of the Columbia River Gorge—stark views of snowcapped volcanic mountains, excellent whitewater and wind, and an easy pace of life. There were only a couple of wineries in the area at the time and little competition for a remote property that included twelve acres of Riesling. Complete with a mesmerizing view of Mount Hood, a large barn, and an A-frame house big enough for the young family, it was ideal for the Goodwillies.

The couple retrofitted the barn to house winemaking operations and a small, comfortable tasting room with an expansive deck (and, later, a space for their son to practice the drums). The deck fills up quickly during the summer, when guests gaze at Mount Hood and bask in the sun for hours; a pass-through window to the tasting room allows for effortless refills. High in the hills of Husum, the winery is sheltered from the wind and removed from the rhythms of town. The serpentine dirt road leading to Wind River makes reaching your destination a bit of an adventure—and weeds out less intrepid visitors.

Wind River promises more than sweeping vistas and rustic appeal. Though the winery produces just three thousand to thirty-five hundred cases each year, it offers a dozen varieties of wine, including the little-known Lemberger and two show-stopping dessert wines: a late-harvest Chenin Blanc called Finale, and Port of Celilo, a deep, rich port named for its vineyard of origin.

---

94   **WIND RIVER CELLARS** // 196 Spring Creek Road, P.O. Box 215, Husum, WA 98623

T 509.493.2324
E info@windrivercellars.com

www.windrivercellars.com

ACCESS
About 15 minutes from Hood River. From Interstate 84, take exit 64. Head north on Button Bridge Road and continue over Hood River Bridge ($0.75 toll). Turn left onto Highway 14 and go 1.5 miles. Turn right onto Highway 141 Alt and go about 2 miles. Bear left at Highway 141 and go about 4.5 miles to Husum. Turn left onto Spring Creek Road and follow signs to the winery.

Hours open for visits and tasting: 10AM–6PM daily, except major holidays and the last two weeks of December.

TASTINGS & TOURS
$5, waived with bottle purchase.

Tours: No regularly scheduled tours. Occasional special-event tours. Appointment necessary.

Typical wines offered: Pinot Noir, Merlot, Cabernet Sauvignon, Merlot, Tempranillo, Lemberger, Syrah, Chardonnay, Pinot Gris, Riesling, Gewürztraminer, Port of Celilo, and Finale (late-harvest Chenin Blanc).

Sales of wine-related items.

PICNICS & PROGRAMS
Picnic area open to the public on the deck. Picnic ingredients sold in tasting room. Cheeses, crackers, salami, breads, and dipping oils are available in summer. Catered lunches and dinners for groups of eight or more with advance reservations.

Special events: Frequent events throughout the year, including Annual Chili Cook-off, Reds Release Party, and Fondue in February; Fungi with the Fun Guy Mushroom Festival in April; Wine and Herb Festival in May; Memorial Weekend Open House; Running with the Bulls Celebration of Tempranillo in June; Harvest Celebration Weekend in September; Thanksgiving Weekend Open House.

Wine club.

When the Goodwillies started Wind River, they made a commitment to use only grapes grown in the gorge, in addition to the Riesling from the 1980 vineyard on site. The couple forged a relationship with Rick Ensminger of nearby Celilo Vineyards, a vineyard winemakers throughout the Northwest hold in high esteem for its exemplary old-vine Gewürztraminer and Chardonnay. Over time, the Goodwillies contracted fruit from other vineyards, including Horse Heaven and small plots in Skamania County.

They have added wines to their portfolio in an organic, seemingly haphazard manner. On one occasion, a pear grower told Joel he was considering tearing out part of his orchard to plant vines. Joel suggested Tempranillo, the robust Spanish varietal that has thrived in Oregon's Umpqua Valley. Today Tempranillo is Wind River's top seller. Another time, Horse Heaven asked the Goodwillies if they could use some Chenin Blanc because Hogue Cellars had discontinued the wine. Joel wasn't overly enthused, but he asked the vineyard manager if it was possible to get the grapes super-ripe. The experiment led to the late-harvest Finale, a delightful sipper that smells like honeysuckle in summer.

Young and gutsy, the Goodwillies place a premium on fun. They sell 85 percent of their wine at the tasting room, drawing visitors with year-round events that feature not just wine, but also mushrooms, herbs, chili, and homemade chocolate shot glasses to serve port in on Valentine's Day weekend. The winery is small enough that the Goodwillies manage it without much additional help, granting a personal experience to anyone who can make it up Spring Creek Road. ✎

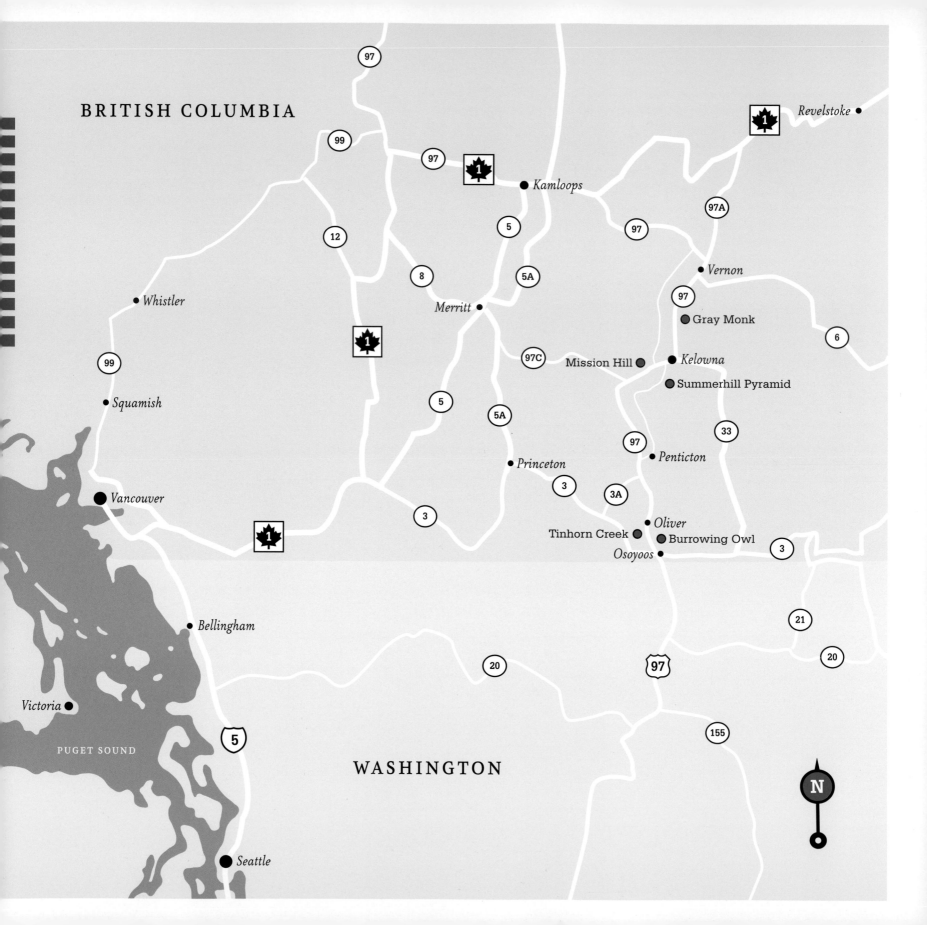

British Columbia

Per capita, British Columbians consume more wine than any other people in North America. Not a bad place to open a winery—and there is no shortage of start-ups. In 1988, just 14 wineries existed in the province, but now it is home to more than 130, with dozens of licenses pending. Still, with only one other growing region—Ontario—in Canada, wineries cannot keep up with domestic demand. National thirst, combined with high export taxes, makes it difficult to find many Canadian wines in the United States, but that provides a great reason to visit.

Our exploration of B.C. wines is limited to the primary wine region, the hypnotic Okanagan Valley. You'll find a mix of large established producers, such as Inniskillin and Sumac Ridge, and tiny fringe wineries with names like Therapy and Blasted Church. And you'll find much more than ice wine. Though Canada enjoys a reputation for crafting superior ice wine, it also suffers from being pegged as a one-trick pony. Winemakers are experimenting with a host of grape varieties, intent on demonstrating the valley's versatility as a growing area. Chances are, you'll be able to speak with winemakers directly when you stop by to try their Chardonnay and Merlot, a benefit of visiting this youthful region. ❧

THE WINERIES

Burrowing Owl Estate Winery

Gray Monk Estate Winery

Mission Hill Family Estate

Summerhill Pyramid Winery

Tinhorn Creek Estate Winery

Don't tilt your head skyward hoping to spot a soaring owl—you're more likely to see one scurrying rapidly on the ground, if you spy one at all. The endangered pint-sized bird that lends its name to this southern Okanagan winery travels mostly by foot, not wing. It makes its home underground in burrows dug by marmots and badgers, or in the drainpipes installed by the Burrowing Owl Conservation Society of British Columbia. Spend some time at the winery, which features an interpretive display on the native bird and supports species reintroduction

and habitat enhancement efforts, and you'll be eager to take up the cause.

The urge to protect the winsome owl, forced out by ranchers who depleted the marmot and badger population to preserve their pastureland, is emblematic of the changes to the Black Sage Bench. McIntire Bluff to the north, the rocky Osoyoos Band to the east, and the Okanagan River define this unusual microclimate. In the past decade, vineyards have largely supplanted ranchland: the Golden Mile, a stretch of land running along Highway 97, now boasts the largest concentration of vineyards and commercial wineries in the province. Though the nearby town of Oliver retains a blue-collar edge, it is also home to white-tablecloth restaurants and is the self-proclaimed Wine Capital of Canada.

Jim and Midge Wyse were among the first to take a chance on the sun-baked sandy soil, acquiring a hundred sagebrush-strewn acres in 1993. Jim, a developer in Vancouver, was fishing around for a new business opportunity when he noticed an ad for a winery in the area. Though the Wyses didn't end up purchasing that particular winery, Jim became hooked on the idea and soon bought the land that would become Burrowing Owl Vineyards.

Jim planted the acreage with four varietals: Chardonnay, Pinot Gris, Merlot, and Cabernet Sauvignon, a grape few thought would receive enough hot sunshine to ripen properly. But prolonged daylight exposure—the region receives two more hours of

daylight than California's Napa Valley—and winters tempered by warm air traveling inland from the Pacific proved naysayers wrong. The Cab performed beautifully, and Jim added another Bordeaux grape to the lineup: Cabernet Franc. After establishing healthy vineyards, Burrowing Owl began making wine as well, producing its first vintage offsite in 1997 and completing its own production facility in 1998.

This measured approach to empire building serves Burrowing Owl and its fans well, treating consumers to superb handcrafted wines and a rich winery experience. Perched in the center of a tidy patchwork vineyard, the modernist Mission-style winery got its most recent update in 2006, seeing the addition of a ten-room guesthouse and an expanded restaurant and wine bar. The ample inn matches the elegant, boxy architecture of the winery facility and provides visitors with the opportunity to witness firsthand the rhythms of a vineyard. The chic, seasonally focused Sonora Room restaurant moved from the winery building to the guesthouse, offering lunch and dinner spring through autumn and serving an in-room breakfast to overnight guests. A swank library room designed to host VIP tastings was the final touch, providing a venue for sampling aged Burrowing Owl wines.

The new restaurant and tasting room echo the design details of the original space, which include slablike distressed-fir counters, decorative ironwork crafted by a local blacksmith, and exquisite hand-stenciled ceiling beams that lend a vaguely Moroccan flair. The Wyses transformed the old tasting room into a more casual wine bar, serving tapas in the grand light-filled room and adjoining balcony.

Though eating, drinking, and lounging in the sun (or poolside) are top draws at Burrowing Owl, further exploration of the property rewards the curious wine enthusiast. If you miss one of the twice-daily guided tours offered on weekends, hike up the bell tower and study the interpretive installations on staircase landings. Topics range from barrel making to barrel aging, and the stairway tour provides views of the cavernous concrete cellar, fermentation tanks, and the vineyard grid, where different varietals are distinguishable by leaf color.

Informed tasting-room pourers are happy to answer questions about Burrowing Owl and its wines,

---

BURROWING OWL ESTATE WINERY // 100 Burrowing Owl Place, R.R. #1, Site 52, Comp 20, Oliver, BC V0H 1T0

T 877.498.0620; 250.498.0620
F 250.498.0621
E info@burrowingowlwine.ca

www.burrowingowlwine.ca

ACCESS
About halfway between Oliver and Osoyoos. From Highway 97 southbound, turn left on Road 9. Travel about 5 kilometers, following signage to the winery. From Highway 97 northbound, turn right on Road 22. Travel about 3 kilometers to the well-marked winery.

Hours open for visits and tasting: 10AM–6PM daily, Easter to late October.

TASTINGS & TOURS
Suggested $2 donation in support of the Burrowing Owl Conservation Society.

Tours: Complimentary guided tours 11AM and 2PM Saturday–Sunday. Self-guided tours of the winery and vineyards available anytime. No appointment necessary.

Typical wines offered: Pinot Gris, Chardonnay, Pinot Noir, Merlot, Cabernet Franc, Cabernet Sauvignon, Syrah, and Meritage.

PICNICS & PROGRAMS
No picnic area open to the public. Sonora Room Restaurant open for lunch and dinner daily, Easter to late October.

Special events: Okanagan Spring Wine Festival in early May; Okanagan Fall Wine Festival in early October.

but touring reveals fascinating tidbits that may contribute to your appreciation of the wine in ways sipping cannot. Burrowing Owl practices sustainable farming, maintaining bat nurseries and bluebird boxes to ward off pests and composting grape stems for future use as fertilizer. It uses only grapes grown onsite, and even maxed out at thirty thousand cases annually, the winery can't produce enough to satisfy demand. (Currently, half of the winery's output lands in Vancouver restaurants and shops, one-quarter is sold at the winery, and one-quarter is sold online.)

Further edification is found in the field. In 2006, the Wyses introduced a Vineyard Walk to encourage visitors to roam outside and examine different grapes up close. Beginning at the winery building, the route passes through rows of Merlot, Malbec, Petit Verdot, and more; informative signs identify each variety. Visitors are also welcome to hike a perimeter loop that circles all three hundred acres of the vineyard and takes about an hour and fifteen minutes to complete. You might just encounter the bighorn sheep that mosey down the Osoyoos Band—or catch a glimpse of the winery's elusive namesake owl. ❧

Gray Monk Estate Winery

OWNERS: **THE HEISS FAMILY** // WINEMAKER: **GEORGE HEISS JR.**

The Heiss family knew it wanted a life on the farm. The only question was what kind of farm. Luckily for local imbibers thirsty for something more satisfying than jug wine, the pioneering Heisses passed over cattle, chickens, pigs, and even mushrooms in favor of grapes.

And what a farm it is. Though homes are now as common as vines and fruit trees on the hills of Okanagan Centre, the landscape is pastoral, not suburban. Grapes and visitors alike bask in the sun reflecting off serene Lake Okanagan below, a truly breathtaking vista.

Considering that many wine lovers today are amazed that grapes can grow, let alone flourish, in a province with a reputation for long, cold winters, the decision to transform an orchard into a vineyard in British Columbia's northern Okanagan Valley in 1972 was downright radical. But George and Trudy Heiss—émigrés from Austria and Germany, respectively—were ready to make a decisive career shift from hairstyling to grape growing, even without a blueprint for cultivating wine grapes in the region.

On the advice of neighboring growers, George Heiss planted Rosette and Marèchal Foch, cheap, lackluster red hybrids—and promptly ripped out the Rosette upon discovering its blandness. The Marèchal Foch yielded serviceable wine, but it wasn't until 1976 that Gray Monk found its footing, simultaneously applying for a winery license and securing quality vinifera vines— Pinot Gris, Gewürztraminer, and Auxerrois—from a nursery in Alsace.

Visiting Gray Monk, you would never guess the struggles and defeats it endured decades ago. It enjoys consistent traffic year-round and possesses the easy-going confidence of an admired, established elder. The crescent-shaped white stucco winery hugs a hillside amid fifty acres of vines, offering a heart-stopping view of the lake. (Gray Monk recently acquired an additional seven-acre vineyard and contracts grapes from some two hundred acres elsewhere in the valley.)

Modest in comparison to newer blockbuster wineries in vogue across the region, the winery has a well-loved, lived-in feel characteristic of family operations. Founders George and Trudy now run the winery with their three sons. George participates in winemaking but has passed down lead vintner duties to George Jr., while Trudy, gregarious, frank, and funny, is still very much the face of Gray Monk. In fact, there's a good chance that Trudy will be your tour guide, starting visitors off with a video detailing Gray Monk's vineyard-to-crush-to-bottling production cycle. Tours proceed downstairs to check out the crush pad and fermenting tanks, offering guests a glimpse of everything that goes into a great bottle of wine.

Of course, proof lies on the palate, so tours conclude in the homey tasting room–cum–gift shop, where guests can sample several wines free of charge (only those interested in trying ice wine, a labor-intensive wine that's expensive to make, are asked to pay a fee). Time your visit to take in lunch or dinner at the onsite Grapevine Restaurant, or, at the least, treat yourself to sweeping views of the vineyards and lake from the outdoor deck.

A display in the chic library room (used for private events) chronicling the evolution of Gray Monk's label design serves as a micro-history lesson. Its first label, busy with heavy Germanic lettering and an illustration of a jolly monk, brings to mind European ales more than fine wine. Next to this bottle sits a series of successive

---

100 **GRAY MONK ESTATE WINERY** // 1055 Camp Road, Okanagan Centre, BC V4V 2H4

T 800.663.4205; 250.766.3168
F 250.766.3390
E mailbox@graymonk.com

www.graymonk.com

ACCESS
About 25 kilometers north of Kelowna. Take Highway 97 north toward the Lake Country district. Turn left onto Berry Road and follow the Winery Route signs to Camp Road.

Hours open for visits and tasting: 10AM–5PM daily, April–July and September–November; 9AM–9PM daily, July–September; 11AM–5PM Monday–Saturday, noon–4PM Sunday, November–April.

TASTINGS & TOURS
No charge for tasting, except nominal charge for ice wine.

Tours: Hourly 11AM–4PM spring through fall, 2PM daily in winter. No appointment necessary.

Typical wines offered: Chardonnay, Pinot Blanc, Pinot Gris, Pinot Auxerrois, Riesling, Gewürztraminer, Siegerrebe, Gamay Noir, Pinot Noir, Merlot, Cabernet Sauvignon, Rotberger, Ehrenfelser Icewine, Ehrenfelser Late Harvest, Kerner Late Harvest, Sparkling, Latitude 50 Series proprietary blends.

Sales of wine-related items.

PICNICS & PROGRAMS
No picnic area open to the public. Grapevine Restaurant open for lunch and dinner seasonally.

Special events: Okanagan Spring Wine Festival in early May; live music events throughout the summer; Okanagan Fall Wine Festival in early October.

redesigns, straight on through to the current incarnation, a tasteful black-and-gold affair with a prominent "G" wreathed in vines.

Like the morphing labels, Gray Monk has grown increasingly sophisticated, compounding the experience it has gained with each harvest, rising to craft captivating wines such as its tight, dry Auxerrois, a white in the Pinot family; its supple, peach-tinged Siegerrebe, a wonderful aperitif or dessert sipper; and its ultra-popular Latitude 50, a smooth red blend. (The wine is named for Gray Monk's proximity to the 50th parallel—three minutes and nineteen seconds north, to be precise—the same latitudinal band that runs through grape-growing zones in northern France and Germany's Rhineland.)

Gray Monk built its reputation on its white wines—all of which are fermented and brought to maturity in stainless steel tanks instead of oak barrels—because those were the only vines it could obtain in the beginning. It turned out that white varietals were well suited to the cool climate of the Northern Okanagan, which is tempered by the moderating effect of the lake. Using grapes grown farther south in sun-absorbing sandy soil, Gray Monk has also enjoyed tremendous success with red varietals, including Merlot, Pinot Noir, and Cabernet Sauvignon. Trudy says that demand is so great that the winery could easily double its maximum production of seventy thousand cases and still sell out. "To this day, we're still playing catch-up. We sell every bottle of every varietal—we really filled a need because the wines here in the '60s and '70s were so bad." But doubling production would change the timbre of a family-run business so close-knit that Trudy's mom still bakes for the crushing crew. And in an industry that relies on feel as much as chemistry, the personal touch counts for a lot. ✆

Mission Hill Family Estate

OWNER: ANTHONY VON MANDL // WINEMAKER: JOHN SIMES

Mission Hill Family Estate was designed to blend into Okanagan Valley's Westbank hillside, its concrete buildings cast in warm terra cotta hues to mimic the burnished mountains surrounding Lake Okanagan. But to suggest that Mission Hill disappears into the landscape is like saying Las Vegas blends into Nevada.

The big-bucks estate is a complete stunner. Everything is crafted to convey quality and longevity—you can see it in the heavy doors made of salvaged railroad ties and in the restrained tasting bar. Proprietor Anthony von Mandl purchased the site in 1981 with the desire to produce world-class wines and thrust British Columbia into the league of greats. Regional winemakers agree that Mission Hill helped put the Okanagan Valley on the map.

While the wines consistently receive accolades, it is the winery that is unforgettable. The first indelible image hits you as you walk from the parking lot toward the winery: a wide stone arc gracefully beckons. At its apex is a keystone carved with the von Mandl family crest. As you stroll past a prim rose garden and under the arch, another architectural heavyweight commands your attention: at the opposite end of the courtyard, looming over a lawn that could serve as a bowling green, stands a twelve-story bell tower. Its four cast-bronze bells, also bearing the von Mandl pelican, clang vigorously twice a day.

Mission Hill offers three in-depth tours, which variously include wine tasting with a sommelier and Riedel glasses to take home, but the standard "Five Vineyards" option satisfies the curiosity of most. Corresponding

with the overall grandeur of the place, tours commence in the Chagall Room. *Animal Tales*, the last of twenty-nine tapestries done on direct commission by the Russian-born painter, dominates the intimate gallery. Look for a rooster strutting in the lower left-hand corner of the vivid artwork: the rooster can also be seen on the label Marc Chagall painted for the 1970 vintage of Château Mouton Rothschild Bordeaux.

Visitors progress to the adjacent theater for a short video narrated by von Mandl. The sleekly furnished theater also hosts cooking classes: the screen lifts to reveal a fully equipped kitchen. Next it's back outside for a quick peek through an oculus, a small round window, at the underground caves. (The winery's signature Bordeaux-style blend bears the name of this spylike device.) Knowledgeable wine educators pause to describe architectural details, making tours more than just a quick jog through a winemaking facility.

A trip down to the barrel cellar stands out as a highlight. Roman arches and rough rock walls accentuate caves chiseled out of the earth thirty feet below ground. An imposing vault, secured by an arty iron gate and a menacing padlock, holds even more unusual assets: Greek, Roman, and Chinese drinking vessels dating back thousands of years, which serve as a reminder that the enjoyment of wine is not a newfound pleasure.

Amid neatly stacked barrels, guides explain how barrels soften tannins, the numbering system used to track barrel contents, and the differences among toast

levels. The educators also shine during tutored tastings at the end of the hour-long tours. Held in a barrel room behind the wine shop, the sampling includes three wines. Before visitors are permitted to press lips to glass, guides demonstrate the steps of tasting, including the acquired technique of pulling air into the mouth to aerate wine. Their demeanor is friendly and unstuffy, assuring guests that there are no wrong answers when it comes to the subjective practice of characterizing wine.

Mission Hill harvests some grapes onsite but reaps the majority of its fruit from vineyards spread throughout the Okanagan Valley, exploiting microclimates in the valley's four major growing regions to produce a wide complement of varietals and blends. The winery's offerings are classified as Five Vineyards, the widely available everyday drinker; a more elegant Reserve tier; and S.L.C. (Select Lot Collection), ageworthy wines made with fruit from designated vineyard blocks and sold only at the winery and a few high-end restaurants. Oculus is Mission Hill's baby, a powerful red made from Merlot, Cabernet Sauvignon, Cabernet Franc, and Petit Verdot.

With its ample courtyard, Old World construction, and heart-stopping views, Mission Hill is reminiscent of a modern abbey or the college campus of your dreams, a place that demands lingering. A story accompanies every room, every vaulted ceiling, and every ornate iron fixture, lending a personal touch to a large-scale operation. Even the washrooms are classy. ૭৯

MISSION HILL FAMILY ESTATE // 1730 Mission Hill Road, Westbank, Okanagan Valley, BC V4T 2E4

T 250.768.6448
F 250.768.2267
E info@missionhillwinery.com

www.missionhillwinery.com

ACCESS
From Kelowna on Highway 97 southbound, cross the floating bridge and continue on 97. Turn left onto Boucherie Road, follow it for 5 kilometers, and turn right onto Mission Hill Road. From points south, take Highway 97 to Westbank, turning right at Gellatly Road. Turn left onto Boucherie Road, follow it for 5 kilometers, and turn left onto Mission Hill Road. Follow the road to the very top, past the winery and into the parking lot.

Hours open for visits and tasting:
Hours vary seasonally, but the winery generally is open 10AM–5PM daily, with extended hours

in summer. Closed Christmas, Boxing Day, and New Year's Day.

TASTINGS & TOURS
$5 for three wines, $3 for two wines.

Tours: Five Vineyards Tour is first come, first served, includes tasting of three wines, and is offered several times each day depending on the season; $7. Reserve Tour emphasizes viticulture and winemaking and includes tasting of five wines and souvenir Riedel wine glass; $17; reservations recommended. S.L.C. Guided Tasting offers tasting of S.L.C. and Library wines with a sommelier in the Estate Room and barrel cellar, and includes three small food pairings; $40; reservations required.

Typical wines offered: Chardonnay, Pinot Blanc, Pinot Grigio, Sauvignon Blanc, Sauvignon Blanc–Sémillon, Merlot, Pinot Noir, Shiraz,

Cabernet Sauvignon, Cabernet-Merlot, Ice Wine, and Oculus (a proprietary blend of Merlot, Cabernet Sauvignon, Cabernet Franc, and Petit Verdot).

Sales of wine-related items.

PICNICS & PROGRAMS
No picnic area open to the public. Dining on premises on the outdoor terrace; open for lunch May to October and dinner mid-June to early September.

Special events: Year-round culinary workshops; frequent winemaking and food pairing seminars; seasonal onsite dinners; multiweek wine courses conducted in partnership with the International Sommelier Guild; Okanagan Spring Wine Festival in early May; Okanagan Fall Wine Festival in early October.

Summerhill Pyramid Winery

OWNER: **STEPHEN CIPES** // WINEMAKER: **JAMES CAMBRIDGE** // ENOLOGIST: **ALAN MARKS**

Within thirty seconds of arrival, it becomes clear why Summerhill Pyramid is the most visited winery in British Columbia. There is, after all, a gleaming four-story pyramid opposite the tasting room, not to mention an enormous sculpture of an inverted Champagne bottle spilling into an outsized flute marking the winery entrance. There's also so-called First Contact, a reconstructed First Nations (native Indian) earth house situated next to a restored pioneer cabin, symbolizing the collision of cultures in the frontier-era Okanagan Valley. Then there is the stunning location: an exposed perch high above serene Lake Okanagan. In short, there's much more to Summerhill Pyramid Winery than wine.

There is a source of Summerhill's idiosyncrasies, and his name is Stephen Cipes, a New Yorker who found success in real estate before changing both his address and his occupation with the purchase of sixty-five vineyard acres in 1986. Generous and passionate, Cipes is a New Age disciple with a serious industrious streak. His recent push toward self-sufficiency for the on-site Sunset Bistro includes establishing an eight-acre organic vegetable and herb garden, raising chickens, and producing goat cheese. It's an ambitious undertaking, but just the latest in the continuous march of Summerhill side projects.

Summerhill isn't a theme park, but it certainly reflects Cipes's inquisitive spirit, and there's no question that it is an entertaining stop on the winery circuit. It's also the only B.C. operation specializing in sparkling wines, and it is the province's largest producer of sparkling and ice wines.

Guided tours lasting about forty-five minutes begin in the vineyard to inform visitors about the unique growing conditions of the Okanagan Valley. Predictability is perhaps the region's greatest strength. The seasons roll by like relative clockwork compared to the capricious weather of Napa Valley, Oregon's Willamette Valley, and northern France. Standing in the rain shadow of the Cascades and Rockies, the Okanagan receives only eleven to thirteen inches of rain per year, and its northern latitude ensures long hours of daylight. The arid climate also wards off pests and diseases. Hillside vineyards feature deep, well-drained soil. And cool nighttime temperatures bolster acidity in the fruit.

These combined factors yield small, intensely concentrated grapes, essential to quality sparkling wine. Cipes recognized this opportunity early on, and though Summerhill produces a wide range of varietals, sparkling varieties (and Riesling) remain the focus. Tour guides describe the time-consuming process known as *méthode champenoise* (or *traditionelle*), in which winemakers induce a second fermentation in each bottle—a laborious step that goes a long way toward justifying the wine's expense. Take a good look at the riddling racks where the fermenting bottles rest: they perform double duty as handsome bar supports in the tasting room.

Tours also cover the production of ice wine, another demanding libation. Grapes are ready for harvest only once frozen on the vine (picking often occurs at night), and grapes must remain frozen hard as marbles when pressed to extract the sweet juices within. Summerhill enjoys steady trade with restaurants in Vancouver and frequent sales to international visitors who favor the honeyed dessert wine as a gift for family and friends back home.

Of course, no visit is complete without a peek inside the pyramid. In addition to barrel aging in an onsite warehouse, Summerhill wines come to maturity in the pyramid, reaping the benefits bestowed by the structure's energy. Cipes believes that pyramids attract a number of forces that have a clarifying effect on liquids, exaggerating both favorable and negative characteristics. "You have to be careful and have confidence in the wine, because the pyramid will draw out *all* the wine's qualities," he says. Though he's the only vintner known to age his wines in a pyramid, he's not alone in his conviction that geometry plays a role in enhancing wine: many modern cellars are modeled on European caves featuring Roman arches, another form of "sacred geometry" believed to benefit wine.

Lit only by a small opening at the apex, the atmosphere inside the pyramid is still and commanding. Don't believe in pyramid power? Try standing in the center of the structure: hold your arms outstretched, palms facing a friend, but not touching. Skepticism be damned, you might detect an undeniable charge in the air, similar to the effect of pushing opposing magnets together.

You don't need to be cosmically inclined to enjoy the fruits of Summerhill's labors. Tours terminate in the handsome tasting room, a narrow space accented by flagged stone flooring and circular iron chandeliers and separated from the adjacent restaurant by shelves well stocked with souvenirs and wine. Both the tasting room and bistro stay open late into the evening, making Summerhill an especially enticing destination during the shoulder season, when many winery restaurants go into hibernation. ✎

SUMMERHILL PYRAMID WINERY // 4870 Chute Lake Road, Kelowna, BC V1W 4M3

T 800.667.3538; 250.764.8000
F 250.764.2598
E info@summerhill.bc.ca

www.summerhill.bc.ca

ACCESS
About 10 kilometers from downtown Kelowna. From Highway 97, head south on Pandosy Street for about 3 kilometers. Continue onto Lakeshore Road for 6 kilometers and head straight uphill on Chute Lake Road.

Hours open for visits and tasting: 10AM–7PM daily, November–March; 10AM–9PM daily April–October. Closed major holidays.

TASTINGS & TOURS
No charge for tasting.

Tours: Complimentary tours offered at noon and 1, 2, 3, and 4PM in summer; noon and 1 and 2PM in winter. No appointment necessary.

Typical wines offered: Brut N/V, blanc de blancs, Pinot Noir brut, Ehrenfelser, Chardonnay, Gewürztraminer, Pinot Blanc, Pinot Gris, Pinot Noir, Cabernet Sauvignon, Cabernet Franc, Baco Noir, Merlot, Meritage, Riesling ice wine, Pinot Noir ice wine.

Sales of wine-related items.

PICNICS & PROGRAMS
Picnic area open to the public. No picnic ingredients sold in tasting room. Summerhill Sunset Bistro open for lunch and dinner daily and brunch Sunday year-round.

Special events: Multiday Jazz Brunch extravaganzas during the Okanagan Spring and Fall Wine Festivals in early May and early October.

Wine club.

Tinhorn Creek Estate Winery

OWNERS: BOB & BARB SHAUNESSY, KENN & SANDRA OLDFIELD, SHAUN EVEREST, AND DAVE JOHNSON
WINEMAKER: SANDRA OLDFIELD

Tinhorn Creek Estate Winery derives its name from a gold mine claim staked on the property in 1895. Today visitors can hike up to the stamp mill used to crush ore from the rocky bluffs over a century ago. The remains of the mill inspired the grand stone archway at the winery's entrance, constructed of rocks removed from the land when the vineyards were sown. Though Tinhorn Creek didn't turn out to be a bonanza for hopeful pioneers, its loamy, wind-protected slopes proved fertile turf for grapes.

To reach Tinhorn Creek, follow an uphill drive slaloming through vineyards, variously golden, green, or barren, depending on the season. It's a fitting approach, as vines are a star attraction here, in contrast to many wineries that are miles removed from their grapes. A miniature demonstration vineyard behind the winery—as informative as a museum display—emphasizes the farming side of winemaking. Laminated markers describe the mechanics of trellising and the role of the lowly milk carton (used to protect young vines from wind, mice, and pests). Placards summarize the grape varieties grown at Tinhorn and reveal the total tonnage each type yields. One sign provides a month-by-month account of vineyard activities, while another breaks down Tinhorn Creek's bottom line: it costs $800,000 to plant, stake, and irrigate all 141 planted acres, not including labor.

This candor is characteristic of Tinhorn partners Kenn and Sandra Oldfield, general manager and wine-maker, respectively. The Oldfields met in 1993 at UC Davis, where Sandra was studying enology and Kenn was enrolled in a crash course in viticulture after he and business partner Bob Shaunessy had set their sights on growing grapes in the Okanagan Valley. The Oldfields are equally committed to producing premium wines and spreading the gospel of the grape. "What we do here isn't secret," Sandra says. "We wanted visitors to be able to see what we're doing and interact with the people making the wine."

With this credo in mind, the winery was designed so visitors can tour the facility unaided but safely, wandering corridors suspended over the fermenting tanks, barrel cellar, and crush pad without coming face to face with a forklift. A white board by the crush area is updated daily, listing the workers' agenda so guests can follow along. The self-guided tour allows you to explore the winery at your desired pace and doesn't interfere with the small staff's rather arduous work.

Completed in 1996, Tinhorn Creek exudes rugged charm appropriate to its location. Framed by fiery sumac trees—which, as you'll learn from the vineyard signage, are good slope stabilizers—the expansive butter-yellow winery building overlooks the river valley and buff-colored mountains beyond. Energetic guests can revel in the panoramic views by trekking two- or ten-kilometer paths that loop past the gold mine ruins—or simply opt for a picnic on the patio adjacent to Tinhorn's welcoming tasting room.

Tinhorn Creek's six varietal offerings range from ubiquitous Chardonnay to tricky Pinot Noir to, weather conditions permitting, ice wine and late-harvest Kerner, a dessert elixir with weighty peach and pear aromas. Merlot and Pinot Gris account for nearly half its forty-thousand-case annual production. Like many unfamiliar with the Okanagan Valley, Sandra initially doubted the region's suitability for growing vinifera grapes. "I honestly didn't think they made wine here," the California native says. "But Kenn knew the potential was there, and I liked the area." The prime growing conditions of the valley have duly impressed her.

Sandra joined Tinhorn straight out of school in 1995, turning out twelve hundred cases of wine from the previous year's harvest. The Oldfields experimented with a dozen varietals to determine which grapes thrive in the microclimate Tinhorn occupies. Tinhorn farms just twenty-two acres onsite, growing most of its fruit on vineyards it owns on the Black Sage Bench, near Burrowing Owl Estate Winery. "The Black Sage soil is really sandy, so it traps in heat. Over on this side, the soil is clay and loam, and we get morning and noon sun, then shade for the rest of the day. We're at a higher elevation, and it's much cooler over here, so whites do really well, especially Gewürztraminer."

The Oldfields have also learned what works well at the winery. A lush green amphitheater carved out of a natural gully has been a big hit, attracting musical acts and Shakespearean players. To serve the needs of tourists, Tinhorn partners are considering transforming a pair of contemporary guest suites into a restaurant. Onsite winery restaurants with ambitious menus are common in the Okanagan Valley, where restaurateurs have been slow to catch on to the demand for cuisine on par with the region's high-caliber wines. That's not necessarily an unfortunate outcome for visitors. Winery restaurants have the advantage of serving library selections unavailable elsewhere and provide an optimal setting for consuming wine: alongside great food. ༄

TINHORN CREEK ESTATE WINERY // 32830 Tinhorn Creek Road, Box 2010, Oliver, BC V0H 1T0

T 888.484.6467; 250.498.3743
F 250.498.3228
E winery@tinhorn.com

www.tinhorn.com

ACCESS
About 4 kilometers south of Oliver's town center. From Highway 97 south- or northbound, turn westward on Road 7 and follow it to the winery.

Hours open for visits and tasting: 10AM–5PM daily, November–April; 10AM–6PM daily, May–October. Closed Christmas, Boxing Day, and New Year's Day.

TASTINGS & TOURS
No charge for tasting. Modest fee to taste Oldfield's Collection wines and ice wine.

Tours: Guided tours by appointment only.

Self-guided tours of winery and vineyard available anytime.

Typical wines offered: Chardonnay, Pinot Gris, Gewürztraminer, Merlot, Pinot Noir, Cabernet Franc, and Cabernet-Merlot.

Sales of wine-related items.

PICNICS & PROGRAMS
Picnic area open to the public on the patio and lawn and in the amphitheater. Picnic ingredients sold in tasting room. A well-stocked deli case and fresh bread are available in high season.

Special events: Several summer concerts featuring touring acts in the amphitheater; many seasonal winery events, including vineyard and habitat tours, barrel tastings, and dinners; Okanagan Spring and Fall Wine Festivals in early May and early October.

Wine club.

Glossary

Don't know the difference between a winery and a vineyard? Don't worry: you're not alone. Here's a crib sheet on the lingo of the vine, plus the lowdown on the types of grapes and wines you'll find in the Pacific Northwest.

Appellation: A legally defined geographic zone, classified as an American Viticultural Area (AVA) in the United States or as a broader Viticultural Area (VA) in Canada. These regions are defined by distinctive topographical features that produce wines with shared characteristics, and they contain more specific subappellations.

Barrel tasting: Winemakers and cellar hands regularly taste wine from the barrel as it ages to check its progress. Critics taste from the barrel as a means of predicting how a wine will taste when it is mature. Samples are retrieved with a wine thief, a glass or plastic pipette (think turkey baster).

Clone: A botanical term referring to an individual vine propagated from a mother plant chosen for its characteristics. There are countless clones of particular grape varieties. A winemaker may select a particular Chardonnay clone, for example, for its distinctive attributes.

Fermentation: Whether it occurs in wine, beer, or gin, fermentation is the conversion of sugar into alcohol using yeast. In winemaking, yeast enzymes turn grape sugar into carbon dioxide and alcohol. For certain wines, winemakers encourage a secondary, or malolactic, fermentation to soften acidity.

Oenophile: A wine lover devoted to the study and appreciation of wines. It is possible to be an oenophile without copping an attitude.

Tasting room: The retail arm of a winery, where consumers can learn about wine styles and winemaking, sample and purchase wines, and attend wine-related events. Tasting rooms may be attached to facilities where wine is made or designed as separate entities, often located in towns that have tourist traffic.

Vineyard: A plot of land that produces grapes; similar to a fruit orchard or vegetable farm. Vineyards are easily identified by their tidy rows of vines, which can be anywhere from knee-high to tree-sized and are often situated on sloping land.

Vineyard manager: Underappreciated and misunderstood by the general public, the vineyard manager is often as revered as the winemaker in the wine world. The vineyard manager's main charge is to cultivate vines that produce great fruit, overseeing trellising, pruning, soil and pest management, and much more.

Vinifera: *Vitis vinifera* is the botanical name of the vine species that yields the grapes best suited to winemaking. There are thousands of vinifera grapes, including the familiar Chardonnay, Cabernet Sauvignon, and Merlot. The Concord grape, of the *Vitis labrusca* species, is an example of a nonvinifera grape.

Vintage: Corresponds with the harvest year. For example, a 2003 Pinot Noir was made with grapes picked in the autumn of 2003. Vintages are relatively consistent in the Northwest, where climate and growing conditions vary little year to year; Oregon's Willamette Valley is an exception.

Viticulture: A branch of horticulture, viticulture is the science, study, and practice of growing grapes—essential knowledge for winemakers and vineyard managers.

Winemaker: The person responsible for transforming grapes into wine, managing the process from grape selection through execution of the final blending of mature wine. A winemaker might be very hands-on or simply an overseer, depending on the size and philosophy of the winery.

Winery: A place where grapes are transformed into wine. A winery includes equipment for sorting grapes, fermenting grape juice, and storing juice as it ages and becomes wine. Many wineries have tasting rooms in which they share their wines with consumers. Some wineries are adjacent to vineyards, while others buy grapes from growers located elsewhere.

110

Cabernet Franc: Winemakers in Washington and British Columbia finally are giving this sassy wine its due, bottling it on its own instead of just using it in Bordeaux-style blends. Cab Franc is lighter-bodied and more acidic than its lauded cousin Cabernet Sauvignon, sporting a heady floral perfume and some green vegetable notes.

Cabernet Sauvignon: The titan of red grapes, Cab Sauv is the predominant grape in Bordeaux and Bordeaux-style blends. Calling to mind dark fruits such as cherries and plums, as well as spices such as cinnamon and pepper, the full-bodied wine is lush and lively on the palate and well suited to cellaring.

Chardonnay: America's favorite white is easy to pronounce and easy to love—except when overoaking transforms it into a butter bomb. Northwest winemakers tend to craft lean, crisp versions with more apple than tropical fruit notes, more nut than vanilla flavor. Many are forgoing oak aging altogether, producing zingy, acidic Chardonnay that pairs beautifully with a huge variety of foods.

Gewürztraminer: An early success story in the Northwest, Gewürztraminer thrives in cool climates. It is the classic wine of France's Alsace region and is revered for its heady aroma and complex spiciness. Those with a balance of acidity and residual sugar make a no-brainer companion to fiery Thai, Indian, and Mexican dishes.

Ice wine: This honeyed dessert wine is both a blessing and a curse to British Columbia. Yes, the area has the climate to produce premier, big-ticket ice wine, but B.C. wants to send word that its growing conditions also yield a host of other fine wines. The juice from ice wine is pressed from overripe frozen grapes—Riesling is common, though any type of grape, even red, can be used.

Merlot: A versatile, approachable wine whose popularity led to ubiquity and a glut of dull, inexpensive bottlings. At its best—and Washington producers generally set the standard—Merlot is supple, juicy, and eminently food-friendly.

Pinot Gris: Second to Pinot Noir, Pinot Gris is the most heavily planted varietal in Oregon, and it's starting to catch fire in Washington and B.C. as well. Citrusy, clean, and light, it's a dead-on summer sipper and pairs nicely with seafood and vegetable-driven recipes.

Pinot Noir: The noble red grape of Burgundy became synonymous with Oregon's Willamette Valley after pioneering winegrowers took a gamble on its suitability—and won. Strawberry and blackberry aromas, low tannins, and silky texture characterize the wine, but it's a tough one to pin down. Its layered complexity piques your palate, but it is also an incredibly easy drinker that complements many foods.

Port: Fortified with brandy, Portugal's gift to cigar-smokers everywhere is making its presence known in the Northwest. Winemakers use Tempranillo or Bastardo grapes to turn out sweet ruby port, which is aged about three years, and smooth, complex tawny port, an expensive delight that is aged ten to forty years.

Riesling: Possessing the sweet-tart loveliness of lemonade and zesty acidity of grapefruit, it's no wonder Riesling is so likeable. The off-dry cool-climate white goes in and out of favor, but, due to Americans' thirst for sugary beverages, it currently enjoys incredible popularity.

Sangiovese: The primary grape in Chianti, this famous Italian export is taking root in Washington soil, especially in the sun-baked Columbia Valley. Northwest Sangiovese tends to be fruitier, lighter-bodied, and less smoky than Chianti, emerging as a fine food-friendly alternative to Merlot and Cabernet.

Sauvignon Blanc: Grassy and sharp, Sauvignon Blanc tastes like spring in a glass. Still a minor grape in North America, this palate-tingling white is deservedly gaining recognition and raves.

Sémillon: A versatile white with a golden hue, Sémillon has good backbone and carries fig and tropical fruit aromas. One of two key grapes in classic white Bordeaux (the second is Sauvignon Blanc), it is gradually building a devoted fan base for its ability to pair with poultry, seafood, and creamy pasta dishes.

Sparkling wine: Champagne, the most famous sparkling wine, hails from the eponymous region in northern France and is traditionally crafted in the labor-intensive *méthode champenoise* fashion, which requires winemakers to induce a second fermentation in the bottle. Northwest producers are hewing to this method, turning out zingy, food-friendly bubbly with pronounced apple and lemon aromas.

Syrah: Less tannic than Cabernet and more intense than Merlot, the noble grape of the Rhône is emerging as a new favorite in the Northwest. It thrives in the hot, dry swaths of southern Oregon and central Washington and partners well with meaty, peppery winter fare.

Viognier: Full-bodied and fragrant, straw-hued Viognier is a high-alcohol wine with limited acidity. A creamy texture and peachy nose make it easy to love and somewhat difficult to pair with food, though rich seafood, coconut-milk curries, and buttery pasta dishes are good candidates. Expect to see more Northwest wineries adopt this varietal.

Resources

VISITOR CENTERS & TOURING INFORMATION

OREGON

**Convention & Visitors Association
of Lane County**
754 Olive Street
Eugene, OR 97401
T 800.547.5445; 541.484.5307
www.visitlanecounty.org

Oregon Wine Center
1200 N.W. Naito Parkway, Suite 400
Portland, OR 97209
T 503.228.8336
www.oregonwine.org

Southern Oregon Visitors Association
1500 E. Main Street
Ashland, OR 97520
T 541.552.0520
www.southernoregon.org

Travel Oregon
610 S.W. Broadway, Suite 200
Portland, OR 97205
T 800.547.7842; 503.223.0304
www.traveloregon.com

WASHINGTON

Columbia River Gorge Visitors Association
P.O. Box 271
North Bonneville, WA 98639
T 800.984.6743
www.crgva.org

**Lake Chelan Chamber of Commerce
& Visitor Information Center**
102 E. Johnson Avenue, P.O. Box 216
Chelan, WA 98816
T 800.424.3526; 509.682.3503
www.lakechelan.com

Seattle's Convention & Visitors Bureau
1 Convention Place
701 Pike Street, Suite 800
Seattle, WA 98101
T 206.461.5840
www.seeseattle.org

Tour Grant County
324 S. Pioneer Way
Moses Lake, WA 98837
T 800.992.6234; 509.765.7888
www.tourgrantcounty.com

Tourism Walla Walla
8 S. Second Street, Suite 603
Walla Walla, WA 99362
T 509.525.8799
www.wallawalla.org

Tri-Cities Visitor & Convention Bureau
6591 W. Grandridge Boulevard, P.O. Box 2241
Kennewick, WA 99302
T 800.254.5824; 509.735.8486
www.visittri-cities.com

Washington Wine Commission
93 Pike Street, Suite 315
Seattle, WA 98101
T 206.667.9463
www.washingtonwine.org

BRITISH COLUMBIA

Kelowna Convention & Visitors Bureau
544 Harvey Avenue
Kelowna, BC V1Y 6C9
T 800.663.4345; 250.861.1515
www.tourismkelowna.com

Penticton & Wine Country Tourism
553 Railway Street
Penticton, BC V2A 8S3
T 800.663.5052; 250.493.5812
www.vacationshappenhere.com

Thompson Okanagan Tourism Association
1332 Water Street
Kelowna, BC V1Y 9P4
T 800.567.2275; 250.860.5999
www.totabc.com

Wine Country Welcome Center
34881 97th Street, P.O. Box 10
Oliver, BC V0H 1T0
T 888.880.9463; 250.498.4867
www.winecountry-canada.com

FARMERS' MARKETS

OREGON

Ashland Rogue Valley
T 541.261.5045
8:30AM–1:30PM Tuesday,
March–November

Dundee
T 503.835.0500
9AM–3PM Sunday,
June–September

Hood River
T 541.387.8349
9AM–3PM Saturday,
May–October

Lane County
T 541.431.4923
10AM–3PM Tuesday,
9AM–4PM Saturday,
April–November

WASHINGTON

Chelan Valley
T 509.682.3243
8:30AM–noon Saturday,
June–October

Kennewick
T 509.585.2301
9AM–1PM Sunday,
May–October

Pasco
T 509.531.7274
8AM–noon Wednesday and Saturday,
May–November

Prosser
T 509.786.9174
8AM–noon Saturday,
May–October

Walla Walla
T 509.529.8755
5–9PM Thursday,
9AM–1PM Sunday,
May–October

Woodinville
T 206.546.7960
9AM–4PM Saturday,
March–October

BRITISH COLUMBIA

Kelowna
T 250.878.5029
8AM–1PM Wednesday and Saturday,
April–October

Naramata
T 250.496.5110
4–7PM Wednesday,
June–September

Oliver
T 250.498.0171
9AM–1PM Saturday,
May–October

Penticton
T 250.770.3276
8:30AM–noon Saturday,
May–October

BOOKS

Irvine, Ronald, with Clore, Walter J. *The Wine Project: Washington State's Winemaking History.* Vachon, WA: Sketch Publications, 1997.

Pintarich, Paul. *The Boys Up North.* Portland: Wyatt Group, 1997.

Purdue, Andy. *The Northwest Wine Guide: A Buyer's Handbook.* Seattle: Sasquatch Books, 2003.

Schreiner, John. *The Wineries of British Columbia.* North Vancouver, BC: Whitecap Books, 2004.

Shara-Hall, Lisa. *Wine of the Pacific Northwest.* London: Octopus Publishing Group Limited, 2001.

PERIODICALS

Northwest Palate
P.O. Box 10860
Portland, OR 97296
T 800.398.7842; 503.224.6039
www.nwpalate.com

Oregon Wine Report
P.O. Box 19958
Portland, OR 97219
T 503.452.7030
www.oregonwinereport.com

Vines
159 York Street
St. Catharines, ON L2R 6E9
T 905.682.4509
www.vinesmag.com

Wine Press Northwest
P.O. Box 2608
Tri-Cities, WA 99302
T 800.538.5619
www.winepressnw.com

WEBSITES

avalonwine.com
Regularly updated articles and reviews keep readers informed about the Oregon and Washington wine scene; also, wine can be purchased through Avalon.

oregonwines.com
Search for Oregon wineries by location, name, wines produced, and tasting-room availability.

willamettewines.com
A detailed guide to more than two hundred wineries in Oregon's Willamette Valley, this site also offers lodging, dining, and event information.

winebc.com
The website of the British Columbia Wine Institute includes heaps of information about the region's wines, events, and growing conditions.

winegrowers.bc.ca
This site includes a directory with profiles of the small, lesser-known wineries of British Columbia, billed as the hidden wineries of the province.

113

Directory

Other notable wineries located near the ones profiled in this book. Call ahead for hours.

OREGON

ADEA
26421 N.W. Highway 47
Gaston, OR 97119
T 503.662.4509
www.adeawine.com

Amity Vineyards
18150 Amity Vineyards Road S.E.
Amity, OR 97101
T 888.264.8966; 503.835.2362
www.amityvineyards.com

**Anne Amie Vineyards–
Chateau Benoit**
6580 N.E. Mineral Springs Road
Carlton, OR 97111
T 503.864.2991
www.anneamie.com

Aramenta Cellars
17979 N.E. Lewis Rogers Lane
Newberg, OR 97132
T 503.538.7230
www.aramentacellars.com

Beaux Frères
15155 N.E. North Valley Road
Newberg, OR 97132
T 503.537.1137
www.beauxfreres.com

Bergström
18405 N.E. Calkins Lane
Newberg, OR 97132
T 503.554.0468
www.bergstromwines.com

Brick House Wine Company
18200 Lewis Rogers Lane
Newberg, OR 97132
T 503.538.5136
www.brickhousewines.com

Bridgeview Vineyards
4210 Holland Loop Road
Cave Junction, OR 97523
T 877.273.4843
www.bridgeviewwine.com

Cooper Mountain Vineyards
9480 S.W. Grabhorn Road
Beaverton, OR 97007
T 503.649.0027
www.coopermountainwine.com

Cristom Vineyards
6905 Spring Valley Road N.W.
Salem, OR 97304
T 503.375.3086
www.cristomwines.com

Cuneo Cellars
750 Lincoln Street
Carlton, OR 97111
T 503.852.0022
www.cuneocellars.com

Domaine Serene
6555 N.E. Hilltop Lane
Dayton, OR 97114
T 503.864.4600
www.domaineserene.com

Duck Pond Cellars
23145 Highway 99W
Dundee, OR 97115
T 503.538.3199
www.duckpondcellars.com

Elk Cove Vineyards
27751 N.W. Olson Road
Gaston, OR 97119
T 503.985.7760
www.elkcove.com

Eola Hills Wine Cellars
501 S. Pacific Highway 99W
Rickreall, OR 97371
T 503.623.2405
www.eolahillswinery.com

Eyrie Vineyards
935 N.E. Tenth Avenue
McMinnville, OR 97128
T 503.472.6315
www.eyrievineyards.com

Firesteed Cellars
2200 W. Pacific Highway
Rickreall, OR 97371
T 503.623.8683
www.firesteed.com

Foris Vineyards Winery
654 Kendall Road
Cave Junction, OR 97523
T 541.592.3752
www.foriswine.com

Giradet Wine Cellars
895 Reston Road
Roseburg, OR 97470
T 541.679.7252
www.giradetwine.com

**Griffin Creek at Eden
Valley Orchards**
2310 Voorhies Road
Medford, OR 97501
T 541.512.2955
www.edenvalleyorchards.com

Henry Estate Winery
687 Hubbard Creek Road
Umpqua, OR 97486
T 541.459.5120
www.henryestate.com

HillCrest Vineyard
240 Vineyard Lane
Roseburg, OR 97470
T 541.673.3709

Hood River Vineyards
4693 Westwood Drive
Hood River, OR 97031
T 541.386.3772
www.hoodriverwines.com

J. Christopher Wines
2636 S.W. Schaeffer Road
West Linn, OR 97068
T 503.231.5094
www.jchristopherwines.com

J.K. Carriere Wines
30295 Highway 99W
Newberg, OR 97132
T 503.554.0721
www.jkcarriere.com

Kramer Vineyards
26380 N.W. Olson Road
Gaston, OR 97119
T 503.662.4545
www.kramerwine.com

**Lange Estate Winery
& Vineyards**
18380 N.E. Buena Vista Drive
Dundee, OR 97115
T 503.538.6476
www.langewinery.com

La Velle Vineyards
89697 Sheffler Road
Elmira, OR 97437
T 541.935.9406
www.lavelle-vineyards.com

Melrose Vineyards
885 Melqua Road
Roseburg, OR 97470
T 541.672.6080
www.melrosevineyards.com

Panther Creek Cellars
455 N. Irvine Street
McMinnville, OR 97128
T 503.472.8080
www.panthercreekcellars.com

Paschal Winery
1122 Suncrest Road
Talent, OR 97540
T 800.446.6050
www.paschalwinery.com

Penner-Ash Wine Cellars
15771 N.E. Ribbon Ridge Road
Newberg, OR 97132
T 503.554.5545
www.pennerash.com

Ponzi Wine Bar
100 S.W. Seventh Street
Dundee, OR 97115
T 503.554.1500
www.ponziwines.com

Rex Hill Vineyards
30835 N. Highway 99W
Newberg, OR 97132
T 503.538.0666
www.rexhill.com

RoxyAnn Winery
3285 Hillcrest Road
Medford, OR 97504
T 541.776.2315
www.roxyann.com

R. Stuart & Co.
845 N.E. Fifth Street, Suite 100
McMinnville, OR 97128
T 503.472.6990
www.rstuartandco.com

St. Innocent Winery
1360 Tandem Avenue N.E.
Salem, OR 97303
T 503.378.1526
www.stinnocentwine.com

Silvan Ridge–Hinman Vineyards
27012 Briggs Hill Road
Eugene, OR 97405
T 541.345.1945
www.silvanridge.com

Soter Vineyards
10880 Mineral Springs Road
Carlton, OR 97111
T 503.662.5600
www.sotervineyards.com

Stoller Vineyards
15151 N.E. Stoller Road
Dayton, OR 97114
T 503.864.3604
www.stollervineyards.com

Torii Mor
18325 N.E. Fairview Drive
Dundee, OR 97115
T 503.538.2279
www.toriimorwinery.com

Tualatin Estate Vineyards
10850 N.W. Seavey Road
Forest Grove, OR 97116
T 503.357.5005
www.tualatinestate.com

Van Duzer Vineyards
11975 Smithfield Road
Dallas, OR 97338
T 503.623.6420
www.vanduzer.com

Weisinger's of Ashland
3150 Siskiyou Boulevard
Ashland, OR 97520
T 800.551.9463
www.weisingers.com

WillaKenzie Estate
19143 N.E. Laughlin Road
Yamhill, OR 97148
T 503.662.3280
www.willakenzie.com

Witness Tree Vineyard
7111 Spring Valley Road N.W.
Salem, OR 97304
T 888.478.8766
www.witnesstreevineyard.com

Zerba Cellars
85530 Highway 11
Milton-Freewater, OR 97862
T 541.938.9463
www.zerbacellars.com

WASHINGTON

Abeja
2014 Mill Creek Road
Walla Walla, WA 99362
T 509.526.7400
www.abeja.net

Amavi
635 N. Thirteenth Avenue
Walla Walla, WA 99362
T 509.525.3541
www.amavicellars.com

Barnard Griffin
878 Tulip Lane
Richland, WA 99352
T 509.627.0266
www.barnardgriffin.com

Betz Family Winery
18512 142nd Avenue N.E.
Woodinville, WA 98072
T 425.415.1751
www.betzfamilywinery.com

Blackwood Canyon
53258 N. Sunset Road
Benton City, WA 99320
T 509.588.6249

Buty Winery
535 E. Cessna Avenue
Walla Walla, WA 99362
T 509.527.0901
www.butywinery.com

Canoe Ridge Vineyard
1102 W. Cherry Street
Walla Walla, WA 99362
T 509.527.0885
www.canoeridgevineyard.com

Cayuse Vineyards
17 E. Main Street
Walla Walla, WA 99362
T 509.526.0666
www.cayusevineyards.com

College Cellars of Walla Walla
500 Tausick Way
Walla Walla, WA 99362
T 509.524.5170
www.collegecellarsofwallawalla.com

Dunham Cellars
150 E. Boeing Avenue
Walla Walla, WA 99362
T 509.529.4685
www.dunhamcellars.com

Glen Fiona
1249 Lyday Lane
Walla Walla, WA 99362
T 509.522.2566
www.glenfiona.com

Goose Ridge Estate Vineyards and Winery
16304 N. Dallas Road
Richland, WA 99352
T 509.628.3880
www.gooseridge.com

Hogue Cellars
2800 Lee Road
Prosser, WA 99350
T 800.565.9779; 509.786.4557
www.hoguecellars.com

J. Bookwalter Winery
894 Tulip Lane
Richland, WA 99352
T 877.667.8300; 509.627.5000
www.bookwalterwines.com

Kiona Vineyards Winery
44612 N. Sunset Road
Benton City, WA 99320
T 509.588.6716
www.kionawine.com

K Vintners
820 Mill Creek Road
Walla Walla, WA 99362
T 509.526.5230
www.kvintners.com

Northstar Winery
1736 JB George Road
Walla Walla, WA 99362
T 509.525.6100
www.northstarmerlot.com

Nota Bene Cellars
9320 15th Avenue S., Unit CC
Seattle, WA 98108
T 206.459.2785
www.notabenecellars.com

Patit Creek Cellars
4 S. Fourth Avenue
Walla Walla, WA 99362
T 509.522.4684
www.patitcreekcellars.com

Pepper Bridge Winery
1704 JB George Road
Walla Walla, WA 99362
T 509.525.6502
www.pepperbridge.com

Portteus Winery
5201 Highland Drive
Zillah, WA 98953
T 509.829.6970
www.portteus.com

Rulo Winery
3525 Pranger Road
Walla Walla, WA 99362
T 509.525.7856
www.rulowinery.com

Seven Hills Winery
212 N. Third Avenue
Walla Walla, WA 99362
T 509.529.7198
www.sevenhillswinery.com

Syncline Wine Cellars
307 W. Humboldt Street
Bingen, WA 98605
T 509.365.4361
www.synclinewine.com

Tagaris Winery
844 Tulip Lane
Richland, WA 99352
T 509.622.7999
www.tagariswines.com

Tamarack Cellars
700 C Street
Walla Walla, WA 99362
T 509.526.3533
www.tamarackcellars.com

Thurston Wolfe Winery
588 Cabernet Court
Prosser, WA 99350
T 509.786.1764
www.thurstonwolfe.com

Walla Walla Vintners
225 Vineyard Lane
Walla Walla, WA 99362
T 509.525.4724
www.wallawallavintners.com

Waterbrook
31 E. Main Street
Walla Walla, WA 99362
T 509.522.1262
www.waterbrook.com

Whitman Cellars
1015 W. Pine Street
Walla Walla, WA 99362
T 509.529.1142
www.whitmancellars.com

Woodward Canyon Winery
11920 W. Highway 12
Lowden, WA 99360
T 509.525.4129
www.woodwardcanyon.com

BRITISH COLUMBIA

Bella Vista Vineyard
3111 Agnew Road
Vernon, BC V1H 1A1
T 250.588.0770
www.bellavistawinery.ca

Benchland Vineyards
170 Upper Bench Road S.
Penticton, BC V2A 8T1
T 250.770.1733
www.benchland.ca

Blasted Church Vineyards
378 Parsons Road
Okanagan Falls, BC V0H 1R0
T 250.497.1125
www.blastedchurch.com

CedarCreek Estate Winery
5445 Lakeshore Road
Kelowna, BC V1W 4S5
T 250.764.8866
www.cedarcreek.bc.ca

Hillside Estate Winery
1350 Naramata Road
Penticton, BC V2A 8T6
T 250.493.6274
www.hillsideestate.com

Kettle Valley Winery
2988 Hayman Road
Naramata, BC V0H 1N0
T 250.496.5898
www.kettlevalleywinery.com

La Frenz Winery
740 Naramata Road
Penticton, BC V2A 8T6
T 250.492.6690
www.lafrenzwinery.com

Lake Breeze Vineyards
930 Sammet Road
Naramata, BC V0H 1N0
T 250.496.5659
www.lakebreezewinery.ca

Mt. Boucherie Estate Winery
829 Douglas Road
Westbank, BC V1Z 1N9
T 250.769.8803
www.mtboucherie.bc.ca

Nichol Vineyard & Farm Winery
1285 Smethurst Road
Naramata, BC V0H 1N0
T 250.496.5962
www.nicholvineyard.com

Nk'Mip Cellars
1400 Rancher Creek Road
Osoyoos, BC V0H 1V0
T 250.495.2985
www.nkmipcellars.com

Pentâge Wines
4400 Lakeside Road
Penticton, BC V2A 8W3
T 250.493.4008
www.pentage.com

Poplar Grove Winery
1060 Poplar Grove Road
Penticton, BC V2A 8T6
T 250.492.4575
www.poplargrove.ca

Quails' Gate Estate Winery
3303 Boucherie Road
Kelowna, BC V1Z 2H3
T 250.769.4451
www.quailsgate.com

Red Rooster Winery
891 Naramata Road
Penticton, BC V2A 8T5
T 250.492.2424
www.redroosterwinery.com

Sumac Ridge Estate Winery
17403 Highway 97N
Summerland, BC V0H 1Z0
T 250.494.0451
www.sumacridge.com

Wild Goose Vineyards
2145 Sun Valley Way
Okanagan Falls, BC V0H 1R0
T 250.497.8919
www.wildgoosewinery.com

Index